Chiara Lubich

The Secret of Unity

Chiara Lubich

The Secret of Unity

New City
London Dublin Edinburgh

First published under the title
L'Unità e Gesù Abbandonato 1984
by Città Nuova Roma

First Published in Great Britain under the title
Why Have You Forsaken Me? 1985
by New City
57 Twyford Avenue, London W3 9PZ

© 1985 New City London
This revised edition 1997

Cover design by Duncan Harper
Illustration a particular of Stabat Mater by Ann Devine

A CIP catalogue record of this book available
from the British Library

ISBN 0 904287 54 8

Typeset in Great Britain by
Phoenix Typesetting, Ilkley, West Yorkshire
Printed and bound by
BPC Wheatons Ltd, Exeter, Devon

Contents

Introduction	7
Unity	19
Jesus Forsaken key to unity with God	41
Jesus Forsaken key to unity with our neighbour	92

Introduction

Looking back on the failed coup that effectively ended the existence of the USSR, Boris Yeltsin remarked in 1994: 'I believe history will record that the twentieth century essentially ended in August 19–21, 1991.' Certainly, as we approach the third millennium after Christ, there is a sense that the human family is about to start a new phase in its history — but not necessarily of yet another deep-rooted division, rather of a movement towards a new unity of the human family. To understand better what Chiara Lubich has to say in *The Secret of Unity* it may be useful to fill out its context a little.

1. THE *WHY* OF THE HUMAN QUEST

No matter how far back we go in history, we find that human beings have been questing for attunement to the source of their existence. From the spellbindingly beautiful cave paintings of Australia, some 40,000 years ago, to those of Spain and France 20,000 years back, and right up to our own day, in the sometimes strange and yet fascinating forms of modern music, sculpture, film and painting, this yearning for an order of existence which will lead beyond its disorder, has expressed itself endlessly. On the walls of an almost 20 feet deep shaft in the huge natural cathedral provided by the caves at Lascaux, for example, the early stone age people of about 18,000 BC depicted a cosmic battle between symbols of earth and heaven. Linked with that scene, probably representing the dying days of the world in the depth of midwinter, they painted beside it their hope of rebirth symbolized by a powerful rhinoceros accompanied by six large dots representing, perhaps, their hope of renewal in the first six cycles of the moon, the first six months, of the new year as it reaches towards midsummer. Much later, from 3200 BC to 2000BC, at Ireland's Newgrange, England's Stonehenge, Scotland's Maes Howe, and Wales' Bryn Celli Ddu, we have evidence of our stone age forebears' unquenchable desire to outlast disorder and death. Their massive stone constructions were oriented in hope towards the reordering power of the undying renewal of sun and moon, focusing particularly on midwinter and midsummer sunrise.

When we turn from the mute memorials of our stone age brothers and sisters to the writings of the great Eastern religions, Hinduism, Buddhism, Confucianism, Taoism, Zoroastrianism, we find even more explicitly expressed, the same constant experience — of anguished acknowledgement of human limits, physical and moral, refusal to accept these limits as final, and the hope of achieving a peace beyond the disorder of the world. We've probably come across the Hindu prayer beautifully expressing this, written some 500 years before Christ: 'From the unreal lead me to the real. From darkness lead me to light. From death lead me to immortality.' (*Brhadaranyaka Upanishad*, I, iii, 28) And that quest became philosophy, the love of divine wisdom, in the Greek experience of the disaster of Troy, in the tragic poets' 'wisdom through suffering,' and especially in Socrates' death for the sake of truth.

2. THE *WHY* OF THE DIVINE QUEST

But human history isn't only a matter of the human search for attunement to an order beyond the disorder of the cosmos. One of Abraham Heschel's books was called *God in Search of Man: A Philosophy of Judaism* (1955). The title conveys the radical difference between, on the one hand, the quest for God we can find from the earliest humans up to many of the great Eastern religions and classical Greek philosophy and, on the other, what happens in the Old Testament. What was new for the Jewish people was that God was seeking them out, that they were God's beloved people. A good example is the Book of Job, written perhaps c. 500 BC. Job loses all that is external to him, his children and his wealth, and later what is internal to him, his health, but most profoundly, his inner sense of unity with God. At the end of his quest for that unity to be re-affirmed by God, conveyed by his questioning, Job discovers that all along, God has been in quest of his love for him for his own sake. Finally, he who sought God is entrusted with the task of mediating God to his friends.

3. The intersection of the divine *Why* and the Human *Why*

St Luke tells us that Jesus grew in wisdom. In terms of what we've been saying, that deepening in wisdom could refer to the human quest of Jesus as a human being, who, like us in all things except sin, advanced in his own quest of the mystery of existence. But Jesus is also the Word of God, the revelation of the Father's quest for humankind, and the Answer to all human quests. Nowhere more clearly than in Chiara Lubich's writings has the intersection of these two quests in Christ been explored. In *The Secret of Unity*, she expresses, through experiences, letters, meditation and theological insight, the centrality of the coming together in the one Jesus, God and man, of the humanity's anguished *Why?* to God, and God's loving *Why?* to humanity. But before going a little more into what this book is about, let's continue to set the context for understanding its enormous relevance to our own time.

4. The First Christian Cultures

This new synthesis in the incarnate Word of divine vision and human exploration, expressed in the existence, life, words and deeds of Jesus, is what constitutes the first Christian culture. And that expansion of human to divine culture occurred whenever Christianity took root in human culture, so that the early Church Fathers spoke of finding in those human cultures 'seeds of the Logos,' discovering in them quests or anticipations of the incarnate Word. In fact, the encounter between the Gospel and the Syrian, Coptic, Abyssinian, Greek, Latin, Germanic, Celtic, Slavic, Hungarian, Armenian, cultures, resulted in a flowering of a series of new and beautiful cultural syntheses, where each of these cultures, in their language, their art, their politics, their social ethos, became more or less fully penetrated by the Gospel.

5. The Disintegration of the Christian Synthesis

Very much within the culture of the Christian world, there developed, at a personal level, a notion of the infinite worth of each individual. In art, there was the elaboration of a secular music, architecture, painting, sculpture, literature. In the intellectual area, there emerged a natural science independent of philosophy or revelation. At the political level, the European nation states began to feel the need to assert their freedom from any spiritual authority, at least insofar as it interfered with their political power. Moving on a few centuries, there were the American, French and Russian revolutions, with their more or less violent assertion of independence, no longer just from the Church, but from hereditary monarchy, and a vindication of the rights, first of the middle classes against the aristocracy, then of the proletariat against the middle classes.

None of these developments were necessarily anti-Christian. In fact, historically they could hardly have occurred without the doctrine of the incarnation. That doctrine taught that the humanity of Christ is not absorbed into God, but is reaffirmed in its own, created autonomy, and fulfilled in the Word. Its cultural expression, as we've noted, occurs when a human reality encounters Christianity. Then it's not abolished, but finds a new freedom and fulfilment within the revelation of the Gospel. This had led to an acknowledgement of the dignity of each human person, and of each human society, including a range of developments in the arts and in politics, all of which flowed from an affirmation of the genuine value of secular, created, reality.

The synthesis between the Gospel and a whole range of European cultures, a synthesis conveniently called Christendom, began to break down about 1500 AD. It's difficult to explain why this happened — perhaps, in some ways, it was unavoidable. However, from the time of the late middle ages, Christianity seems not to have been lived at a level deep enough to continue this task of continuing incarnation. And this failure was experienced by some as a blocking off of the emergence of many genuinely secular experiences. An ominous split began to appear, with religion relegated to a purely spiritual domain, while the secular domain developed apace according to its own norms and requirements. Despite attempts, particularly in Protestant Europe, to deal with the secular, on all sides of the divided Church religion came increasingly to be regarded as the business of its specialists and enthusiasts, the clergy, monastic and religious orders, or as purely a private affair divorced from the rules and rational considerations of the real world.

6. The Disintegration of the Modern Synthesis

The gradual rejection of Christianity left the new secular culture searching for its own absolutes — those of the Self, of Nature, Race, Class, History, Nation, Capital, Science, Technology, Sex, Evolution or whatever. This quest for absolutes that are not absolutes led to what may be called the prophetic disappointments of philosophers like Nietzsche, poets like Baudelaire or Larkin, writers like Kafka and Beckett, or painters like Francis Bacon. By now, in these waning years of the 20th century, after the wars of the Isms, both physical and spiritual, none of the great substitute-absolutes that we call ideologies, has any widespread appeal. We've come across the awful scene in Elie Wiesel's *Night*, when a Jewish concentration camp inmate asks, while a young boy is being hanged — 'Where is God? Where is he?' And Wiesel, witnessing the scene, answered within himself: 'Here he is — He is hanging on this gallows.' There is the Italian Marxist philosopher, Massimo Cacciari, who declared at a philosophy conference some time ago, 'I think that to speak of man today, we have to think of that cry of Jesus: "My God, my God, why have you forsaken me?"' Or the Russian film director, Andrei Tarkovsky, who said in one of his last interviews, before he died in 1987, 'If Golgotha hadn't taken place, there really would be nothing.'

When he was in Spain in 1982, Pope John Paul II expanded St John of the Cross' understanding of the dark night of the soul to that of a collective dark night of the spirit being undergone by contemporary culture. He found that collective dark night being experienced not only outside, but within the Church, when, referring to the disintegration we have been speaking of, he remarked: 'these trials, these temptations and this result of the European drama, not only question the Church and Christianity from the outside, as a difficulty or external obstacle to the work of evangelization which must be overcome. Rather, in a certain sense, they are internal to Christianity and to the Church.'

7. RE-LIVING THE FORSAKENNESS OF JESUS AS THE WAY TOWARDS BUILDING A NEW CIVILIZATION OF UNITY

The Church's awareness of its own failure to live up to its calling, and the modern culture which was at least in part provoked by that failure, has led to its purification. And the secular world is only too well aware of its own Godforsakenness. So that a convergence from both sides seems to be occurring at this time: the world's rediscovery of its need for the true Absolute, and Christianity's rediscovery, in Chiara Lubich, in Hans Urs von Balthasar and Jürgen Moltmann, of the *Why* of Jesus as the Answer.

What does this mean for the Christian today? In the first place, that my dialogue with modern culture is with the Jesus Forsaken in myself, with my own being too affected by the surrounding culture, my own failure to witness to God-Love, which has been one of the causes of unbelief in the secular world around me. Then that dialogue with Jesus Forsaken within myself will lead me also to embrace all that is negative, and that seems opposed, or at least contrasted to, Christianity, in this world, with its imperfections and deviations.

When we turn to the talks/meditations presented here as *Secret of Unity* we will discover a new and very different kind of answer to the present crisis. Not a new philosophy or ideology, although it is giving rise to a new theology — rather it's a way of living, so close to the bone that it's impossible, reading the text, not to be confronted by the question of how, concretely, should I become a builder of unity. The talks, in a way, take a circular route. The first one, on unity, explains precisely what Chiara Lubich means by unity. Then, the second two talks, 'Jesus Forsaken key to unity with God,' and 'Jesus Forsaken key to unity with our neighbour,' in effect set out what are the sources of that unity, and how we can achieve it.

What's communicated here is nothing less than a lived theology of the Unity/Trinity of God, attained by living Jesus Forsaken. Because by living Jesus Forsaken, we'll be participating in the internal dynamic of Trinitarian life, a dynamic where, through becoming nothing, each person is capable of building unity with, and becoming one with the other. Because inability to reach out to the other person or society as different has characterized the various Isms we are now trying to leave behind, Chiara Lubich's way of living Jesus Forsaken is by no means only a way of individual asceticism, but is also a practicable answer to the crisis of our times.

In *The Secret of Unity* she grounds the three

dialogues — between Christians, with the non-Christian religions, and with all persons of good will — in our being prepared to live Jesus Forsaken and Risen. Not only does she outline how each of us can get beyond our personally experienced limits by embracing them in the One who has himself undergone equivalent limits, but also how each Christian Church can go beyond the specific disunity it experiences towards a unity of all Christians. And towards unity with the non-Christian religions, Judaism, Islam, Hinduism, Buddhism, all of which have their own profound anticipations of the experience of Jesus Forsaken and Risen. And because Jesus Forsaken is the One who is without God, by opening ourselves to him, identifying ourselves with him, we can reach out to him in the third dialogue, to all those of good will, whether or not they are believers.

Finally, Chiara Lubich suggests how, loving the face of Jesus Forsaken in all the needs of contemporary society, in all those who are suffering the effects of the modern disintegration, we can, through the such broader movements as New Families, New Humanity, and more recently, of Youth for a United World, find ways to make these dialogues concrete, in collaboration with all who also desire genuine personal autonomy and genuine solidarity. Because at the heart of all our dialogues is our love of the One whose quest was derailed into Godforsakenness, and Who, through loving beyond that apparently absolute lostness, found a way to a new and deeper oneness with his Father — not just for his own humanity, but for all humanity.

Brendan Purcell

Unity

As we can all see, the world today is characterized by many tensions: tensions between East and West, between North and South; tensions in the Middle East and in Central America; wars, the threat of new clashes, the explosion of acts of terrorism and other evils typical of our times. Yet, despite all of these tensions, the world tends towards unity. It is a sign of the times.

This is expressed, for example, in the Christian world by the Holy Spirit who urges the various Churches and ecclesial communities towards re-unification after centuries of indifference and conflict. It is expressed by recent Popes, like Paul VI whose teaching is full of the idea of unity, and now by John Paul II who is the personification of this idea, with his journeys all over the whole world and his universal love which embraces all peoples.

It has been expressed by the Second Vatican Council, the documents of which constantly return to this idea. Subsequently, it has been expressed by the establishment of the Vatican Secretariats: for the unity of Christians, for dialogue with other religions and with all people of good will.

It is expressed by the World Council of Churches.

This same tension of the world towards unity is expressed even by ideologies which we cannot share, but which also attempt to solve the tremendous problems of the age in a worldwide manner. It is expressed too by international bodies and organizations – in the same way as the modern means of communication favour unity by drawing all the world into a single community or a single family.

Yes, this tension towards unity exists in the world. And it is in this context too that we must see the Focolare Movement and its spirituality.

In fact, whenever we are asked how our spirituality can be defined, and what is the difference between the gift that God has poured out on our Movement and the gifts with which he has adorned and enriched others in the Church in our times and in the past, we do not hesitate to say: unity.

Unity is our specific vocation. Unity is what characterizes the Focolare Movement. Unity and not other ideas or words which may, in some way, sum up other divine and splendid ways of going to God, as 'poverty' could for the Franciscan movement, or 'obedience', perhaps, for the Jesuits, or 'the little way' for those who follow St Thérèse of Lisieux, or 'prayer' for the Carmelites following St Teresa of Avila, and so on.

Unity is the word that summarizes our spirituality. Unity, which for us contains every other supernatural reality, every other practice or commandment, every other religious attitude.

If, however, unity is our typical vocation, let us return for a while to the beginning of our forty-year long history, to when it was set alight like a flame, so that we can still keep it alive in our hearts or rekindle it if need be. Let us recall some things that occurred and read again the written records we have kept about this idea. A rapid review of all this will help us to remain faithful disciples of the priceless gift that God has given us.

To begin with, let us relive a well-known event of the very earliest days. It was during the war. A few girls and I were in a dark place, maybe a cellar. We were reading Jesus' last will and testament (John 17) by the light of a candle. We read it all through with ease. One by one those difficult words seemed to be lit up. It seemed to us that we understood them. We felt, above all, that here was the *Magna Carta* of our new life and of everything that was about to be born around us. After a little while, when we became aware of the difficulty, if not the impossibility, of carrying out such a programme, we felt urged to ask Jesus for the grace of teaching us how to live unity.

Kneeling around an altar we offered our lives to him so that, if he wished, he could bring about unity. As far as we remember, it was the feast of Christ the King. We were struck by the words of liturgy that day: 'ask of me, and I will make the nations your heritage, and the ends of the earth your possession.' (Ps. 2:8)

We had faith and asked.

Later on, with joy and wonder, we linked these events and our aspiration to achieve unity with the encyclical that was promulgated by Pope Pius XII in 1943, the very year of our Movement's birth: the encyclical *Mystici Corporis*.

In our hearts one thing was clear: unity is what God wants from us. We live to be one with him and one among ourselves and with everybody. This marvellous vocation binds us to heaven and immerses us in a universal family. Nothing could be greater. For us, no ideal excels this.

Let us go back again to the early days. It was thought to be a good idea that every morning I should give a brief meditation to the group of my first companions in the hall called *Sala Massaia*. We met at seven o'clock in the morning. I felt an inner urge not to hinder the Holy Spirit with my own thoughts, who, if he thought it useful, would illuminate me. For this reason I prepared myself by prayer, declaring my nothingness and that God was all: 'I am nothing, you are everything,' I would repeat many times before Jesus in the Blessed Sacrament. After having prayed like this, I would jot down some notes. And it was with this method in particular that God formed the first group of us in the new ideal.

Of the notes written during those years one set remains, probably from 1946. They dwell on just one subject, the one which most interested the Movement that was being born: unity.

The style is extremely concise, as notes are in general. Having spoken of the need for us to be another Jesus, they make a clear statement of the programme that God has for us.

'The soul must, above all else, keep its gaze fixed on the one Father of many children. Then look at all persons as children of our Father. With thought and with the affections of the heart always go beyond every limit imposed by a [merely] human life and tend constantly, and because of an acquired habit, to universal brotherhood in one Father: God'.

And the notes continue:

'Jesus, our model, taught us just two things, that are one: to be children of our Father and to be brothers and sisters of one another.'

Further on a virtue is highlighted, one which is essential for our unity with God and our neighbour, and which in his letters St Paul points to when he exhorts Christians to love one another in order to build up unity.

'Virtue,' say the notes, 'that unites the soul to God . . . is humility, becoming nothing. The tiniest speck of the human which does not allow itself to be assumed by the divine breaks unity with the gravest consequences. The unity of the soul with God, who dwells in it, presupposes total self-annihilation, the most heroic humility . . .

'Unity with other souls is reached, moreover, by

means of humility: aspire constantly to the "first place" by putting ourselves as much as possible at the service of our neighbour.

'Every soul that wishes to achieve unity must have only one right: to serve everyone because in everyone it serves God . . .

'Like St Paul: though free make ourselves slaves of all to gain for Christ the greatest number. (cf. 1 Cor.9:19)

'The soul who wishes to bring unity must keep itself in a constant abyss of humility so as, for the sake and service of God in its neighbour, even to lose its own soul.

'It does not enter into itself except to find God and to pray for its brothers and sisters and for itself.

'It lives constantly "emptied" because utterly "in love" with the will of God . . . In love with the will of our neighbour that it wishes to serve for God! A servant does only what the Master commands.'

And in the following thought can be glimpsed the tremendous revolution that this ideal can bring about:

'If everybody, or even a tiny group, were the servants of God in their "neighbour", soon the world would belong to Christ.'

Loving our neighbour like this, in fact, we reach reciprocal love, unity – Jesus' last will and testament accomplished, as the end of the notes state.

At that point, it is made clear who our neighbour is: our neighbour is the brother or sister who passes us by in every moment of the day. We must love that person in such a way that Christ is born, grows, develops in him or her.

'The important thing is to have a single idea of our "neighbour".

'Our neighbour is the person who passes us by in the present moment of our life. Always be ready to serve him or her because in that person we serve God. [Have a] simple eye [which means] to see one Father, to serve God in our neighbour; to have one neighbour: Jesus.

'The simple eye sees "a potential Christ" in everyone. It puts itself at the service of all so that Christ may come to life and grow in them. It sees in each person a Christ who is born, who must grow, must live, doing good – as a new child of God – and who must die, rise again and be glorified . . .

'The soul can give itself no rest until – through its constant service – it discovers in its neighbour the spiritual outline of Christ.

'For this reason, since Christ lives in it . . . it serves Christ in the neighbour so that he may grow in age, wisdom, grace . . .

'And that is why the soul will accomplish its Ideal (the only ideal of Jesus): *Ut omnes unum sint* – "May they all be one" – when it uses the present moment for the service of the neighbour.'

Our ideal, then, is to realize the prayer that Jesus pronounced on the evening of Maundy Thursday.

On that evening, having instituted the Eucharist, instituted the priesthood and given the New Commandment to his disciples, he went outside, down some stone steps, as tradition tells us, towards the stream called Kedron: 'May they all be one' (cf. John 17:10,21,22).

All one. Until all are one, those 'all' that Jesus certainly intended, the Movement can have no respite. This is the end for which we were born, the purpose for which he brought us into being.

No other motives were present in our minds in those early times.

The idea of ecumenism for example, was far from our minds; we had no knowledge of it. Even years later when, around 1950, I went to visit the Jesuit priest, Father Boyer, the founder of the *Foyer Unitas*, I replied firmly 'No!' when he asked me whether unity, as we understood it, was meant to contribute towards the unity of the Church. God had not yet revealed to us his plans in this direction.

Unity. But what is unity?

In these same notes from 1946 we find a certain explanation, expressed as yet in terms learnt at school:

'We must not form a mixture, but a compound, and this will come about only when each one will lose himself in unity in the heat of the flame of divine love.

'What is left of two or more [persons] who "form a compound"? Jesus – the One . . .

'When unity passes by, it only leaves one trace: Christ.'

And here, in a letter from 1947, is a definition of unity, given after experiencing it:

'Oh! Unity, unity! What divine beauty!

'We do not have human words to say what it is! It is Jesus.'

Then in a letter from 1948, we read:

Unity!
Who would dare speak of it?
It is ineffable like God!
You feel it, see it, enjoy it but . . . it's
    ineffable!
Everyone rejoices in its presence, everyone
    suffers from its absence.
It is peace, joy, love, ardour, the atmosphere
    of heroism, of the highest generosity.
It is Jesus among us!

Unity, therefore, is Jesus.

Yes: unity is Jesus. When he had risen he declared: 'I am with you always, to the end of the age.' (Matt. 28:20) Unity is one of his presences in the Church, together with his presence in the Eucharist, in his Word, in those who have the duty to spread the gospel, in those who have to govern the community, in the poor in whom he hides himself . . .

And we are called to live unity in every moment of our daily life. As we have been able to intuit it is brought about by serving our brothers and sisters. But what is the best way of practising this service? Right from the first years it was clear to us that it could be done well by 'making ourselves one' with every neighbour we met.

Often, even now, we are carried away by work, by haste, by the desire perhaps to do the will of God, we fall into doing what appears to us to be God's will yet in reality is not.

Before anything else God wants this from us: that we make ourselves one with the person who is next to us, with the one who journeys through life with us, the one whom we come to know day by day, also – as is possible – through the media: television, radio, newspapers ... above all, with the person who suffers and the one who is without God.

We read in the notes from 1946:

'We must be one with our neighbour, not in an ideal way but a real one. Not in a future way but in the present.

'To be one and that is to feel in ourselves the feelings of our neighbours. Deal with their problems as something belonging to us, made ours by charity. To be them. And this for love of Jesus in our neighbour.

'To melt the bindings of this hard heart of stone and have a heart of flesh to love other people'.

When during the early times, God taught us the

way of living that he had planned for us, we practised 'making ourselves one' with others for a long time.

It is not easy. It demands the complete emptiness of ourselves: the removal of ideas from our heads, of affections from our hearts, of everything from our wills in order to identify ourselves with others.

When I speak with someone who wishes to be part of the Movement and to confide in me, since answers would come to me immediately, at length I practise putting aside my own ideas, until the other person has completely emptied the fullness of his or her heart into mine. In doing this I am convinced (also because experience had taught it to me) that in the end the Holy Spirit suggests exactly what I should say. Emptying myself, in fact, I love, and if I love, he manifests himself (cf. John 14:21). I have experienced thousands of times that if I had interrupted the person who was speaking half-way through, I would have said something that was not right, not illuminated, that was merely 'human'. Whereas, allowing through love the other person to make his or her worries enter into me, I can then give the answer that clears up everything.

And should this way of loving, this way of mutual penetration be established between two people, then the unity is achieved which brings Christ among us.

If we are called to unity, our way to go to God must, then, pass through our neighbour. It is by means of that passageway, at times as dark and as murky as a tunnel, that we arrive at the light. This is the mysterious path that God asks us to follow in order to reach him.

He wants us every day, every hour, to perfect this art which at times is exhausting and wearisome, but always marvellous, full of life and fruitful, this art of 'making ourselves one' with others: the art of loving

It is the cross to which we must nail ourselves every day: our particular cross *par excellence*. It is life for us and for those whom we love – and, if it is mutual, it is life among us. It is Jesus.

The Ideal of our life, right from the beginning, was God. And he came down and comes down to live in the midst of us by means of unity, because 'Where charity and love are, there is God'[1] and, 'Where two or three are gathered in my name, I am there among them.' We find God in unity. It is the main place where a focolarino,[2] and whoever chooses this way, meets God. Only if we find him there do we have

---

[1] From an ancient hymn.
[2] Focolarino: a member of a focolare house. Here it is used in the masculine form, which in Italian can, as in the present case, include the feminine. Plural: focolarini. When only the feminine is intended the word is focolarina. Plural: focolarine.

the grace to meet him fully in the Eucharist, in the Word, in the Hierarchy . . . because he illuminates us about all these supernatural realities.

It is wonderful, and still today something truly astonishing, to see how Jesus urges us, from the time when the Movement took its first steps, to stress very forcefully what St Peter said: 'Above all maintain constant love for one another' (1 Pet. 4:8). .

Yes, because this is the novelty of the good news: before everything else continual, mutual charity. Charity as the basis of everything, the soul of everything, the only thing able to give value to everything.

In a letter dated 1948, addressed to a group of religious who had understood and received the gift God had given to the Movement, we find written:

'. . . before everything else (even if this "everything else" includes the things which are the most beautiful, the most sacred: like prayer, like celebrating Holy mass, etc., etc.) be one! Then it will no longer be you who act, pray, celebrate . . . but always Jesus in you!'

Unity must be maintained at all costs. Indeed, it costs death, but it gives that life which is Jesus. And it is this life, which triumphs over our death and is our reward, that gives life to the world through the communion of saints, through the witness it offers, through the strength it gives, so that we can face the world, and every disunity in it, and offer a remedy for it.

Another letter from 1948 says, 'May everything collapse. But unity – never!

'Where there is unity there is Jesus! . . .

'And do not fear dying. You have already experienced that unity demands the death of everybody to give life to the One!

'Upon your death lives Life!

'The Life that, without your knowing it, gives life to many souls. As Jesus said, "*Pro eis, sanctifico me ipsum!*" – "For their sakes I sanctify myself" (John 17:9). To bring about the unity (of your town) and of the world, be united among yourselves.

'It is the only way.

'That unity, in which Love lives, will give you the strength to face every outward disunity and to fill every emptiness . . .'

Elsewhere it is written:

'I would like all the world to collapse, but that he should always remain among us . . .

'God has given us an ideal . . . Let's remain faithful to it, cost what it may, even if one day we should cry out with our soul in flame because of infinite pain: "My God, my God, why have you too forsaken me?" . . .

'If we stay faithful to our charge (*Ut unum sint* – may they be one) the world will see unity . . . All will be one, if we are one!

'And do not fear giving up everything for unity; without loving . . . beyond all measure, without losing your own judgement without losing your own will, your own desires, we will never be one! Wise is the one who dies to let God live within! And unity is the training ground for these warriors of the true life against the false one . . .

'Unity above all else! Discussions count for little, even the most sacred questions, if we do not give life to Jesus among us'.

As mutual love is a commandment for Christians, so unity is our first duty. The statute of the focolarini demands unity as the rule of every other rule: Jesus among them before anything else.

This duty, however, brings with it a joy that is new and full, the joy promised by Jesus, 'so that they may have my joy made complete in themselves' (John 17:13).

Joy, which is one of the gifts God gives to unity, is a richness of which today perhaps we are not sufficiently aware. Just as physically you do not feel your health, while you notice pain, the same happens with joy in the supernatural life. It is of the very nature of a truly Christian life, and maybe for this reason it is not stressed very much. Nevertheless, it is a very special gift, one to be ardently desired.

Let us look at the world around us: how much apathy, boredom, sorrow, craving and how many mad extremes in search of happiness! What is the drug problem, what is the intoxication with the cinema, with television, and what are the political uprisings in the world? And wars too? They are a thirst for peace, for justice, for happiness. The human heart is made for joy.

Very well, God has revealed to Christians, and to us focolarini today, where the source of joy is, the place where it may be mined.

Because the focolarini live unity, they are happy. Because the focolarini bring unity, they are dispensers of joy.

We have always said that joy is the uniform of a focolarino; and the gift a focolarino must give to the world is happiness.

There are those who are called to give bread and shelter or advice or instruction or housing . . .

The focolarini give joy, with or without all these other things, which depend upon whether 'making themselves one' with their neighbours demands giving food or drink; finding a job for another person; visiting them; bearing with others or simply sharing with them.

In any case, we are called to give comfort, peace, light and especially joy: to make the world smile.

In the first days of our new life, this new joy made us exult – we wished to share it with everyone and we were grateful to God for having given it to us. Speaking to Jesus, a letter says:

'The happiness that we experience in the unity

that you have given us by your death, we wish to give to all the souls who pass next to our souls! We can't keep it just for ourselves, because many . . . hunger and thirst for this fullness of peace, this infinite joy! . . . Tear open our heart . . . all our being, so that you alone live within us! . . . We have chosen as our all You on the cross, in the maximum forsakenness, and you give us heaven on earth! You are God, God, God.'

We must thank God for this joy, even though we must not become attached to it, but use it as a launching pad to bring unity in the world.

'Do this (maintain unity),' (this dates from 1948) 'as a sacrosanct *duty*, even if it will bring you immense joy!

'Jesus promised the fullness of joy to whoever lives in unity! . . .

'Enjoy your unity, but for God and not for yourselves . . .

'Let's make unity among us the springboard for running ahead, . . . to where there is no unity in order to build – unity!

'Indeed: as Jesus preferred the cross for himself rather than Mount Tabor, let us also prefer to stay with whoever is not in unity, so as to suffer with them and be certain that ours is pure love!'

Unity is 'making ourselves one' with our neighbours.

And when there are no neighbours with us? When we have to work alone or rest or relax or study?

As we all know: all immersed in the will of God in the present, the one will of God which is different for each of us, we all become the will of God. And since the will of God and God coincide, we are living our being-God-by-participation, and thus we are one with him and among ourselves.

I remember that ever since 1947 one method we used to build unity was precisely the carrying out of God's will as a concrete expression of our love for him.

In a letter to the first focolarine we read:

'Fix just one idea in your head.

'It was always one sole idea that made the great saints.

'And our idea is this: unity. (Unity with God): "Yes, Father!"

'Let's repeat in every present moment to his will: "Yes, Father!" Yes, yes, yes, always and only yes. This will make you participate in our unity that exists only in God.

'His will binds us and consumes us in him and among ourselves . . .

'Unity: I want what he wants . . .

'Unity: constant direct communion with God, with the radical mortification in the present moment of all that is not God. I only want God . . .

'Unity: among us, in this marvellous community of souls spread throughout the world, locked and enclosed by the love of God alone!'

Unity, therefore, is our ideal and nothing else. And this has to be underlined today too, and much more today than in the early times. At that time following the urgings of the Spirit, the thing was clear. Now it is obvious to the focolarini and to those other members of the Movement we call internal. Without doubt unity is lived in the focolares and likewise, I hope, in the nuclei of the volunteers, in the gen units and so on.[3] But in the wider Movement? Among all the others?

Is there not the danger that in certain places our Movement, rather than appearing as the Movement of unity, could seem to be one that only lives and spreads the Word of Life?[4]

Living the Word is an excellent thing, but this too must be done within the reality of unity.

---

[3] The volunteers, short for 'Volunteers of God' are members of the Focolare Movement who are particularly committed to bringing the spirit of the Gospel into society. They meet regularly in small groups called nuclei. The gen, short for 'New Generation', are the young people of the Movement. They meet in small groups called units.

[4] It has been the custom from the beginning of the Movement (1943–45) to choose a word of the Gospel which is applied in each person's daily life for a specific period (usually a month). The intention of this is to re-evangelize oneself. To assist the living of the Word of Life, as each word chosen is called, a commentary by Chiara Lubich is published throughout the world in the Movement's magazines, such as *New City* and *Living City*, and on separate leaflets.

Unity before all else.

Thus if we believe that our ideal can be expressed in the 'choice of God' we are mistaken, because this is present in all spiritualities. St Francis, St Catherine, St Dominic, St Ignatius and all the saints have made the choice of God.

If we think, then, that our spirituality is centred around the 'will of God', we still do not have the right idea. All the saints have 'willed' the will of God.

And if we assert that we must follow the pathway of love, we have still not grasped the distinctive feature of our spirituality. Even the New Commandment of Jesus is underlined by other spiritualities, and consequently is not sufficient to define our vocation.

We must choose God as he wishes to be chosen, loving him, that is, by realizing in practice his last will and testament. We must do his will, which for us is unity; we must love, making ourselves one with our neighbours; we must love one another, but to the point of being consumed in one. We must embrace Jesus Forsaken who, as we will see later, is the key to unity and has thus to be loved with unity in view. We must live the Word of Life after having first of all established continual mutual charity among us and as a way of further nourishing this charity.

Living the Word was certainly something of a novelty when we began, but it was rather the fact of putting our experiences of it into communion, in order to evangelize and sanctify ourselves together, that characterized our Movement.

The Word too is, therefore, at the service of unity, because unity is the culminating point of Jesus' thoughts, summarizing and forming a synthesis of his commands. This is what Jesus has always made us understand. Before all else God wants from us, as the Focolare Movement (that was once called the Movement of Unity), that everywhere we bring to life living cells, with Christ in our midst; cells that are ever more ardent, ever more numerous. God wants from us that we light bigger and begger fires in families, in offices, in factories, in schools, in parishes, in monasteries and convents, to feed the blaze of the love of God in the Church and in society. It is not for nothing that we are called 'focolarini' (bearers of fire) and the places where we live 'focolares' (where the fire burns). Only by acting in this way are we sure of being on the right track, even though in some places or nations we are like a 'little flock' (cf. Luke 12:36), but one which is always his, which is authentic, and is oriented to *ut omnes*, 'may they all be one'.

This is the only way of ordering our Movement, an order which we must establish or return to if we are to hope to have every blessing from God.

Besides, right from the beginning God's programme for the Movement has been this: to make contact with our own environment, becoming perfectly one with our neighbours while, at the same time, remaining open to all the others.

'Your first responsibility,' says one of the letters already quoted, 'is that all your brethren be one, without excluding the other neighbours the Lord puts at your side. You must die . . . completely in Jesus among you! Have everything in common . . . then, one by one, Jesus will draw into unity those who live next to you and prepare for unity those who are far away.

'Just as any object that passes by a whirlpool in the sea or in a lake is sucked irretrievably into it (the suction is caused by the meeting of two currents! . . . Isn't this too a symbol of unity?), so each person who meets Jesus (the Jesus who is among us) will be irretrievably lost in his love.

'I send you my wishes that Jesus among you cast his nets into the great world of your Order and that daily the catch may be miraculous!'

On earth we live as part of the Church militant. We cannot wage a war without weapons and without an objective. Our weapon is Christ who lives in our most perfect unity. The objective: 'May they all be one'.

We cannot but consider each person we meet as a candidate for unity: without doubt God wants to see him or her in the Church perfectly consumed in one with all our brothers and sisters. This is Jesus' dream.

Jesus Forsaken
Key to Unity with God

I

Earlier on, we began to explore in depth the characteristic point on which our spirituality hinges, namely *unity*, and we sought to grasp the first dazzling flashes of this divine idea when it appeared at the beginning of the Movement. And from it we have drawn the joyful and uplifting conviction that, if unity is what God wants from us, then by fulfilling our vocation the Risen Lord is alive in our midst, in the midst of the world in which we live.

We have, therefore, committed ourselves during all this period to setting alight this divine presence among everybody in our meetings, in our various conferences, in every form of community life, often remembering the first counsels of the Holy Spirit, the first ideas that flowered in our mind for the realization of unity.

This in-depth exploration of unity has been such a gift, such an extremely important clarification of the characteristic charism of the Movement, that it brought about a general conversion in us, like a sort of death and resurrection. It is certain that we cannot go any further ahead without continuing always to do all our part to merit the constant presence of the Risen Jesus in our midst.

Now, we would have liked to have gone back over our entire history to see how this idea of unity has been the background or has accompanied, and is the aim of all our pathway. We would have liked to see how it animates all our spirituality, the forms of our life, the ordering of the whole of the Movement, its various structures and the very vows of those who are consecrated to God; and to see how it is stated as our general and specific goal. But we have seen how it is not good to release ourselves from what seem to us to be the demands of the Holy Spirit who if he has announced to us our characteristic spiritual way right from the beginning, has also, right from those times, revealed to use the key to achieving it.

Indeed, if urged by a legitimate desire, but also by the Church's advice (which invites religious families and movements to return to the times when the Holy Spirit give them life, in order to safeguard the genuineness of their inspiration), if, then, we look at the beginnings of the Movement, we can see that a model, a figure, a life was presented to us even before we had any ideas about the way of accomplishing unity. It was the life of the One who knew truly how 'to make himself one' with all people who were, who are and who will be; he who brought about unity, paying for it with the cross, with his blood and his cry; he who gave to the Church the fruit of his presence as the Risen Lord for always, to the end of the world: Jesus crucified and forsaken.

The reality of Jesus Forsaken and our understanding of who he is, preceeded every other thought also in order of time. In fact, if we hold, and rightly, that the beginning of our history was on 7 December 1943 (the date of my consecration to God), we must remember that on 24 January 1944, Jesus Forsaken had already presented himself to our mind and heart.

But let us proceed in proper order.

As when we spoke of 'unity' so as to look more closely at Jesus Forsaken and the first ideas we had about him, we will try to recall episodes and circumstances, and to read the brief writings that have survived. These are facts and thoughts which are already well known, but it is necessary to review them today as well, to make a further analysis of the subject.

A first episode was the meeting with Jesus Forsaken in Dori's[5] house, a meeting which this time we will leave her to tell.

She says, 'We used to go to visit the poor and probably from one of them I caught a skin infection

---

[5] Dori Zamboni, one of the first focolarine.

on my face. I was covered with sores and the medicines I was given were unable to stop the disease. However, with my face carefully protected, I carried on going to Mass, and to our meetings on Saturdays.

'The weather was cold, and it could have been dangerous to go out in it. Because my parents in consequence forbade me to do so, Chiara asked a Capuchin priest to bring me Communion. During my thanksgiving after Communion, the priest asked Chiara when, in her opinion, Jesus suffered most during the passion. She replied that she had always heard that it was the agony he had suffered in the garden of Gethsemane. But the priest said, "I believe instead that it was his suffering on the cross, when he cried out, 'My God, my God, why have you forsaken me?'" (Matt. 27:46; Mark 15:34)

'As soon as the priest had left, having heard Chiara's words I turned to her, sure she would give me an explanation. Instead she said, "If Jesus' greatest suffering was when he was forsaken by his Father, we will choose him like this as our Ideal and will follow him in this way."

'In that moment the conviction that Jesus with his face in torment, crying out to the Father was our ideal, became impressed in my mind and in my imagination. And my poor facial sores, that appeared to me like shadows of his pain, gave me joy because they made me a little like him. From that day onwards Chiara often, indeed always, spoke to me of Jesus Forsaken. He was *the* living character in our existence.'

Let us go on now to a second episode, and together with it to a practice of those early days.

As I have said on other occasions, the aspects of the new life that was about to be born often emerged through actual events. Thus, making a 'bundle' of all our belongings, as we called it, which consisted in putting together the few, poor items of clothing we had, was the beginning of our way of living poverty and of the use we should make of goods.

Our 'putting the books in the attic', on the other hand, signalled the start of a new way of knowing.

Putting aside the word 'apostolate', which was misunderstood at the time, was the start of the spreading of God's love rediscovered.

A letter written only out of obedience, inviting forty people we did not know to a meeting (following a method which seemed to us to be artificial, the symbol of 'non-relationship') was the premise for that outpouring of letters which was the first link between the people who were part of the Movement which was being born.

Likewise, getting rid of all the furniture from our little house, keeping nothing more than mattresses placed on the floor, gave rise to a new kind of interior decoration that was simple and harmonious; and it was, at the same time, the start of our characteristic form of spiritual life. It was on that occasion, in fact, that we hung on the wall just one object: a picture of Jesus Forsaken, as a sign that he alone had to be the one treasure of our existence. Every morning, upon waking, we expressed this decision with the briefest of prayers: 'Because you are forsaken' to which we added, turning to Mary: 'Because you are desolate.'

A single choice, therefore, a radical one: Jesus Forsaken.

The letters of the time underline this:

'Forget everything . . . even the things which are most sublime; let yourself be dominated by only one Idea, by only one God, who must penetrate every fibre of your being: by Jesus crucified.' (21 July '45)

'Do you know the lives of the saints? . . . (They) were just one word: Jesus crucified; . . . the wounds of Christ, their rest; the blood of Christ, the healing bath for their soul; the side of Christ, the jewel box that was filled with their love.

'Ask Jesus crucified, by his agonized cry, to give you the passion for his passion.

'He must be everything for you.' (21 July '45)

Jesus Forsaken was the only book we wanted to read.

'Yes, it's true, I'm doing a university course, but no book, however beautiful or profound it may be, gives my spirit such strength and especially such love as Jesus crucified.' (7 June '44)

And again:

'But above all learn from one book . . . from the crucified Jesus, who was abandoned by everybody! who cries out: "My God, my God, why have you forsaken me?" Oh! if that divine face contracted by a spasm of torment, those eyes reddened but which look at you with goodness, forgetting my sins and yours that had reduced him to this state, were always before your gaze!' (30 January '44)

And in the following years, from time to time, this radical choice was renewed.

A letter dating from 1948 says:

'Forget everything in life: the office, work, people, responsibilities, hunger, thirst, rest, even your own soul . . . in order to possess nothing him! This is everything . . . to love as he loved us, who went so far as to experience being forsaken by his Father for our sake.' (14 August '48)

And in 1949: 'I have only one Spouse on earth, Jesus Forsaken. I have no God but him.'

Therefore, we know him alone. We only wanted to know him. The Spirit repeated in us: 'I know only Christ and him crucified.' Our love for him was exclusive: it allowed no compromise.

The choice of God which had characterized the first step in our new life became precise – to choose God for us meant: to choose Jesus Forsaken.

And here we must pause.

In the same way that we feel the need to give the correct orientation to the Movement wherever it may be on the earth, by reviving the ideas and recalling the intuitions of the early times (for it must always be a Movement for unity and not only, for example, a Movement to live the Word of God better), so also, by returning to the first inspirations, we realize we should emphasize that our choices should not be two; the choice of God and the choice of Jesus Forsaken, but one: *the choice of God in Jesus Forsaken*. In him there is the God-Love whom we have chosen; in him there is the will of God for us; in him there is the possibility of living out the New Commandment, with, that is, the measure of love it requires. He is the Word *par excellence* that Jesus sowed on the earth when he gave life to the Movement. It is Jesus Forsaken lived who is the possibility, the only possibility, of having Jesus among us. It is by loving him that we will manage to be 'another Mary'. By loving him we contribute effectively to bringing about Jesus' last will and testament. With him we will truly live the Church. With love for him we will give space in our heart, and in the hearts of many, to the Holy Spirit.

All of this must be clear.

It is only with love for Jesus Forsaken that we will be able to avoid errors in laying foundations, for example, in relationships between persons which develop at the beginning of this new spiritual path, because of a too human interpretation of the love that the Ideal, God-Love, demands.

In fact, since one's ideas are not very clear in the beginning, inexperience can make one think of and practise love for God and for our neighbour, and also mutual love, mainly as an effusion of feelings.

Undoubtedly the heart of Jesus knew special feelings. We know this. But he manifested his love above all by sacrificing himself on the cross and in his forsakenness.

Jesus Forsaken is our style of love.

He teaches us to annihilate everything within us and outside us, in order to 'make ourselves one' with God; he teaches us to silence thoughts, and attachments, to mortify our senses, even to put aside our inspirations in order 'to make ourselves one' with our neighbours, which means to serve them, to love them.

And the radical nature characteristic of our choice of Jesus Forsaken in the early times, our seeing nothing but him, comes to us today too as a message, as a clear and pressing invitation to make a renewed choice of him as the one love of our life. It reaches us as a warning not simply to embrace all the sufferings which come as a meeting with our beloved and long-awaited Spouse, welcomed always, straightaway, with joy[6] but to contemplate in him the measure of our love for our neighbour –

---

[6] This refers to a spiritual practice, wide-spread in the Movement, that emphasizes the Christian way of embracing suffering.

a measure without measure in the duty to give everything, holding back nothing for ourselves, not even the most spiritual of things, not even the most divine. We have to imitate him in his manner of loving, in the heroic practice of all the virtues that love contains.

The question comes to us: today, do we truly have him alone in our hearts? Or is his place taken, even for brief periods of time, by our self, or by people, activities, jobs, studies or things, in the midst of which we must live, nonetheless, in order to carry out the will of God?

Jesus Forsaken was the one book we read. What did the Holy Spirit make us read there?

We immediately contemplated in him *the summit of his love because it was the climax of his suffering*. In Jesus Forsaken, in fact, *all* the love of a God is revealed.

A letter from January 1944 (just a week after the meeting with Jesus Forsaken) says:

'Joys will come for you, pains and anguish will come. But if you force yourself to see Jesus as I am presenting him to you, and will always present him to you, in the *climax of suffering*, which is the summit of love.' (30 January '44)

And in another letter:

'. . . everything is there. It is *all* the love of a God.' (7 June '44).

And again:

'Do you realize that he has given us *everything*?

What more could he give us – a God who, out of love, seems to forget to be God?' (8 December '44)

Consequently, we realized from the beginning, with endless gratitude, the immense gift of our call to follow him:
'You don't know how fortunate we are to be able to follow this forsaken Love!
'He, in his inscrutable designs, has chosen us among thousands and thousands of people to let us hear his cry of anguish: "My God, my God, why have you forsaken me?"' (8 December '44)
And, looking through the writings we still have, one has the impression that this love of Jesus Forsaken entered, penetrated, and exploded in our hearts like a fire that devours everything, that spares nothing, like a divine passion that overwhelms and envelops heart and mind and strength: like a flash of lightning that illuminates. We saw. We understood. There were rivers of light.

For example, Jesus Forsaken illuminated for us the place that suffering has in the divine economy.
'Jesus converted the world by the word, by his example, by his preaching, but he transformed it by the demonstration of this love: the cross.' (1944)
We discovered his love completely unfolded in him, in his immense suffering, and this vision

inflamed our hearts and urged us too to give value to our personal suffering as an expression of our love for him and, to become in him, with him co-redeemers.

'Just think . . . God came on earth, only once, and that one time he was man and let himself be put on the cross! For me this thought gives great strength to accept with joy that little cross which is always with us.' (1944)

'Whoever knows Love and unites their sufferings to those of Jesus on the cross, losing their drop of blood in the sea of the divine blood of Christ, has the most honoured position for a human being: to be like God who came on earth: redeemer of the world . . .' (1944)

'Believe me, one minute of your life on that sick-bed, if you accept the gift of God with joy, is worth more . . . than all the activity of a preacher who speaks and speaks and only loves God a little' (1944)

'He has infused a great passion into my heart: it is him crucified and forsaken!

'He who from the height of the cross says to me ". . . everything that was mine I have extinguished . . . everything! I am no longer beautiful; no longer strong; here I have no more peace; up here justice is dead; knowledge is unknown; truth disappears. All that remains is my Love, which wanted to pour out *for you* my riches *as God* . . ."

'He speaks to me thus and he calls me . . . to

follow him . . . It is he who is my passion!' (25 December '44)

'Before him every suffering seems to me to be nothing and I await suffering, large or small, as the greatest gift of God, since it is this which is the proof of my love for him!' (7 June '44)

We did not only see in Jesus Forsaken the summit of love, not only was the place of suffering in the divine economy revealed to us, but in him we contemplated the secret of sanctity.

'Do you remember St Rita? In the dark background of her room, where her two children slept, there was the crucified God-Man. He was the secret of her love. He and he alone.

'From that cross came to her the example of patience, of forgiveness, of love lasting and tenacious to the point of death and death forsaken!

'He it was who guided her along the highest ways of sanctity, because before all others Rita loved Jesus crucified.' (1948)

And since we discovered all these riches of his, we saw him as the precious pearl that God offered us. His was a love so sublime, so extraordinary (it had reduced him for us to a 'worm of the earth', to 'sin'!) that it convinced us that no-one would ever be able to resist him. His love is so immense that it could never be repaid!

'Oh! We have found, yes, we have found the precious pearl!

'Oh! Our Love!

'Oh! That man, that "worm of the earth" ... He is "ours"!

'The soul who has found him leaves everything to embrace him! And like the bride in Song of Songs it too goes in search of its treasure and loves him and *adores him*!

'What lover would fail to be drawn by such a love?

'I would like to run through the world and gather hearts for him, yet I realize that all the hearts in the world would not be enough for a Love as great as God!' (15 June '48)

Finally, to conclude with a truly singular illumination.

It was during the first year of our experience when the Spirit showed us Jesus Forsaken as the rule for a new life. A letter from 1944 says:

'As God, he has made of that cry the rule of a new life according to a new ideal.' (8 December '44)

It was, therefore, a new spirituality that the Holy Spirit was raining down on the earth. It was a new ideal to which we were the first to be called.

As time passed the matter became ever more clear: God calls us to Unity (we have listed previously the signs of this vocation) and Jesus Forsaken is the secret of unity. He is the condition for accomplishing Jesus' last will and testament: 'May they all be one'.

In 1948, in a letter to a group of young religious describing our experience we state, not without surprise, that there is a connection between Jesus Forsaken and unity with God and among human beings.

'I have experienced that every soul that is in the front line in Unity and for Unity, is only able to sustain itself upon the basis of a Suffering – Love as strong as that of Jesus Forsaken.' (1 April '48)

'It is for this reason, brothers, that . . . we have taken as the sole aim of our lives, as the one goal, as everything, Jesus crucified who cries out: "My God, my God, why have you forsaken me?" It is Jesus in the greatest suffering! Infinite disunity . . . to give us perfect unity, which we will reach relatively here on earth and then perfectly in heaven.' (1 April '48)

And another letter, to a religious, says:

'Try . . . to embrace him.

'If I had not had him in the trials of life, this way of unity would not exist – unless Jesus had wanted to raise it up in the same form in other places.

'He, forsaken, has won every battle in me, even the most terrible ones.

'But we must be mad with love for him, who is the synthesis of all the sufferings of the body and of the soul: the medicine . . . for every suffering of the soul.' (23 April '48)

Jesus Forsaken, hence, is the key of the charism, the

secret of unity. With him we will always be able to go ahead. It will be necessary to bear this in mind for the future, when, in the difficult moments that can and must come, we could be assailed by doubt about whether things will go forward as before. In these moments it will be good to recall this first light, this extraordinary experience.

II

We finished the first meditation on Jesus Forsaken by trying to understand all that we contemplated, in him, after he had appeared to us.

Now we will read nearly the whole of a letter written to a Gen-Re[7] in 1948, a letter which has as its motto: 'My God, my God, why have you forsaken me?' In it we can already find the most important affirmations about Jesus Forsaken, which explode with great clarity and strength: it is a page which we could say sums up our teaching about him.

To begin with it says immediately that unity is truly understood by whoever loves Jesus Forsaken:

'I am convinced that unity in its most spiritual, most intimate, most profound aspect cannot be understood except by the soul that has chosen as its portion in life . . . Jesus Forsaken who cries out "My God, why have you forsaken me?"' (30 March '48)

Following this, Jesus Forsaken is announced as the secret and guarantee of unity.

'Brother, now that I have found in you an understanding of what the secret of unity is, I would like and I would be able to speak to you for days without end. I want you to know that Jesus Forsaken is

---

[7] Gen-Re: the gen who belong to a religious order or congregation.

everything. He is the guarantee of unity. All light on unity flows forth from that cry.' (30 March '48)

The letter states that to choose him means to generate to unity an infinity of souls.

'To choose him as the one aim, the one goal, the destination in your life is . . . to generate to unity an infinity of souls'. (30 March '48)

As it continues the letter states categorically, right from that time therefore, that the spirituality just being born hinges on two points: Unity and Jesus Forsaken. And it speaks of them as the two sides of the one medal.

'The book of light[8] which the Lord is writing in my soul, has two aspects: a page shining with mysterious love: Unity. A page glowing with mysterious suffering: Jesus Forsaken. They are two sides of the one medal.' (30 March '48)

It is understood, furthermore, that this is a new light, we want to protect it in order not to give 'holy things' to those who are not prepared.

'Brother, not everyone understands these words. Let's not give them to just anyone. May the Abandoned Love find himself surrounded only by

---

[8] This expression refers to the fundamental inspiration of the Movement: its spirituality of unity to which the key is Jesus Forsaken (cf. *The General Statutes of the Work of Mary*, part, chap. 3, art. 8, and Pope John Paul II's address to the priests and religious of the Movement on 30 April 1982, published in *Osservatore Romano* 1 January 1982).

hearts who understand him, because they have felt him passing into their life and have found in him the solution to everything.' (30 March '48)

In that period we described Jesus Forsaken as the 'One Utterly Pruned', he who appeared to be wanted by neither earth nor heaven. We said: earth does not want him, neither does heaven; and we concluded: he can be entirely ours.

Because he was uprooted from the earth and from heaven, he brought to unity those who were 'cut off', who were uprooted from God.

Through Jesus, in fact, we gain by losing, we live by dying; the grain of wheat must die in order to bear new fruit; one must be pruned to give good fruit. It is his law, one of his paradoxes. In this way, the Holy Spirit made us understand that in order to realize *ut omnes* ('May they all be one') in the world, it was necessary to consume in ourselves, the forsakenness, and to welcome Jesus Forsaken in disunity.

In 1949 we wrote to some religious brothers, who had not received permission from their superior to be part of such a new Movement:

'Hasn't it been understood yet . . . that the greatest Ideal that the human heart can wish for – unity – is a vague dream and a chimera if the person who wants it does not place as everything in their heart: Jesus, forsaken by everybody, even by his Father? This (your) apparent detachment . . . from your brothers and sisters who outside of the College, fight, live, and suffer for the same ideal as you – isn't it perhaps for you, a little Jesus Forsaken? . . .

'It is only by embracing Jesus Forsaken with all your heart, embracing him who is all a wound in his body and is all a darkness in his soul, that you will be formed in unity . . . *There* is the secret of our Jesus' greatest and final dream: "*Ut omnes unum sint!*" And you and we, made sharers in this infinite Suffering, will contribute effectively to the unity of all the brothers.' (17 February '49)

In reading these first writings we realize what the charism God had given us was aiming at: *ut omnes*. And to reach it a road, a key, a secret was indicated: Jesus Forsaken.

Jesus came to the earth so that all may be one. Jesus on the cross and forsaken has paid for this goal. He wants a hand from us to realize it: the *Opera di Maria*[9] has made this its specific aim. It will be able to achieve it with Jesus Forsaken, in him and through him.

The charism of the Movement came down from heaven with the precise intention of the Holy Spirit to further the cause of Jesus, which the Church as always pursued: *Ut omnes unum sint* – 'may they all be one'. To all the recipients of these letters of the early days one request only was made to commit

[9] The Focolare Movement is also called *Opera di Maria* – The Work of Mary.

themselves for '*ut omnes*'. And it is symptomatic that the first recipients were girls and religious, young people and adults – meaning that for an ideal which concerns everyone, all vocations were mobilized.

There were those who understood and those who did not. But whoever was touched and illuminated by what was written, felt morally committed to '*ut omnes*'.

This love for Jesus Forsaken, having entered us like a fire, naturally urged us to seek him everywhere.

We were aware of him lonely and abandoned in the depths of many human hearts where he dwells through grace:

'When you find yourself in front of a person, whoever it may be, remember that in that heart there is God and he may even be abandoned by that heart . . . who ever remembers (in fact) that they have Jesus in the depths of their heart?' (undated)

We found him in our neighbours because they cost the forsakenness of God.

'Oh! . . . give him the whole of your existence. Give him your will . . . And his will is all in this: Love God with all your heart! Love your neighbour as yourself. Your neighbour . . . Love him . . . and consider that your neighbour's soul is worth the immense Suffering of Jesus Forsaken! Love

him therefore as if he were Jesus Forsaken!'
(11 January '45)

We found him in people who had been abandoned and left on their own because of the war.

'I know that here people are abandoned and that everyone is fleeing. But I don't want to lose them. Jesus has bought them with his blood.'
(9 January '45)

We discovered him in the homesickness of our young hearts because our parents were far away from us.

'I see him there on the cross. He too is homesick and suffering the abandonment by his Father.'
(25 December '44)

We found him in the tabernacle or on the cross.

'I wish I were beside you. I would take you by the arm, leading you to the little church up here, and, drawing you closer to the tabernacle, show you two things. Low down a tabernacle, bare and cold, surrounded perhaps by flowers and candles but devoid of hearts, and inside the living Jesus! That Jesus who is God! and it is he who has created you and given you the beauties of nature and love in your heart . . . that Jesus who, overflowing with love for these people (and among them there is you and me) after dying in that way, desired to perpetuate there in the tabernacle his agonized abandonment!

Then I would say to you: look up, higher, look at the cross with him on it! Tell me if he hasn't loved you! Tell me what he must have gone through when . . . he felt himself forsaken by everyone, waiting there for death, in that agonized condition, not even watched by his Father!' (11 January '45)

We found him in sufferings and in misunderstandings.
  '. . . never, never as now do we feel that the Lord has granted our wishes and that he loves us. We (certainly) weren't looking for the joys that spring naturally from the life of unity, but the cross and, especially, a cry of suffering that exceeds all others: "My God, my God, why have you forsaken me?" . . . [Now our] Ideal is taken as exaltation or fanaticism . . . People point their fingers at us and mock us . . . [but] when everything seems to fail, behold his divine Figure in his agony which imprints itself upon our souls, a unique pledge of the glory to come. Ah! Paradise! Unity there will be perfect.' (7 July '47)

We found him in the poor whom we sought out, in the sick whom we visited, in prisoners, in those who had erred, like unmarried mothers . . .
  Our heart opened out, therefore, to the whole range of the works of mercy which love can invent, works to which the newly born Movement was to be called in different ways in its various branches.

And all those who had, are having or will have the benefit of this love had, have or will have only one name: Jesus Forsaken.

And, in those early times, what was our attitude before Jesus Forsaken?

We were struck deep inside ourselves by his love and we wanted to do something for him absolutely. Not knowing how to behave first, we tried to show him our love which was full of gratitude by consoling him.

'How terrible for me if I should hear you say that you've become lukewarm and that you do not love him, who is everything for us! You haven't abandoned him, have you? I have such a great hope of consoling Love with your two hearts that it would be an immense torment for me if I were to see you plunge back into the life you once led: quite a good life, yes, but without love for God! Tell me it's not like this: reassure me'. (9 January '45)

And we understood that to console him meant to love him.

'Look at him on the cross, deathly pale, uttering an atrocious cry. You know him, because that cry is your life!: "My God, my God why have you forsaken me?" and it implies: "Will you too forsake me?" And you reply with me: "Never, I would rather die".

'My little sister, never forsaking love means: *to love him, to possess love*!'

The verb 'console' which recurs in these letters, this attitude which should be assumed before Jesus Forsaken, could seem today as if it had been taken from popular piety, like something adopted from a traditional spirituality which was still rather mediaeval. The comment could be made, in fact, that Jesus who is now in heaven on the right hand of the Father, does not need our consolation.

But, if we analyse these writings well, we can understand their precise meaning.

If the historical Jesus, in the moment when he was forsaken, was so alive in our hearts as to seem to be present, he was, nevertheless, never thought of as detached from Jesus who was uttering his cry of forsakenness in the Mystical Body, in the humanity of that time and who truly needed our help, our consolation.

'Jesus, so infinitely sorrowful, needs our consolation. What does Jesus, who is so anguished, lack? It's God that he lacks! How can we give him God? By keeping united, we will have him among us and Jesus, who will be born from our unity, will console our crucified Love! That is why we must make our unity grow in quantity of love and of souls! We want the king to grow to great size among us! And then we will go and seek to remedy every disunity, especially since in every disunited soul we hear groaning, more or less powerfully, the cry of our Jesus!' (1 April '48)

To console Jesus Forsaken. Now we could say that we had to reap what he had sown, to bring to fruition all that he had paid for.

We wanted to love him also by sharing his suffering.

'And today too the day which the bombers wanted to make ugly and cruel was spent in loving. I came out of the air raid shelter after six hours. It wasn't cold and my heart was full of Jesus Forsaken, for whom I live and suffer those little pains he gives me to suffer, so that he may no longer be forsaken!' (1 January '45)

We wanted to love him by imitating him. And since his forsakenness told us how his love was total, we considered that if we did not take care also of little things for his sake, we did not love like him.

'But first and foremost Jesus wants my love. And I will be able to love him like this by contemplating him forsaken: he has given himself utterly to me and I must do the same, giving myself totally to him. I can no longer have my own will; my will is his. I will live doing his will most faithfully also in the little things; for, if these are lacking, I have done nothing for him.' (2 June '45)

And as we chose nothing but him, we preferred him to everything else.

'At times the will of God is suffering, is abandonment, is torment. To want it as the one "preference" of the soul is to render indestructible the unity of our soul with God and hence with our neighbour.' (23 April '48)

To console him, to share his suffering, to imitate him, to prefer him: he called us to all of this.

Now let us look at what were the effects of this behaviour of ours: new effects, perhaps never experienced before, which filled us with wonder.

One of the first was the distinct impression of finding ourselves on a supernatural level.

We read in a letter dated 1944:

'I have married him and I have sought to extinguish every other desire for his sake . . . He and his cry of forsakenness have drawn me, Mum, and they have made me rise above everything, with a broken heart. Yes . . . he alone could do this, he who does not make us neglect (most sacred) affections but makes us feel them in the profoundest depths of our heart and then makes us overcome them.' (25 December '44)

Because of this love for Jesus Forsaken we experienced Life, the supernatural life.

'Seek nothing but him, yearn for nothing but him; and when he comes close to your soul embrace him swiftly and find Life there!' (23 April '48)

Love for Jesus Forsaken developed the virtues in our souls, beginning with humility.

'You know how . . . in the inmost depths of my

soul I bear the love for him forsaken and how I would like to make his cry my life, in the most extreme humility . . . His cry is the source of all humility: he, in the ultimate fulfilment of his Divine Mission, is led by the Divine Will to cry out the forsakenment by that Father who was perfectly one with him!' (30 October '45)

Jesus Forsaken loved brought sweetness to the soul, and rest and fire:

'Don't [try to love him] when we can't do anything else because suffering reminds us of him . . . but prefer him always; don't give weight to the joys, to the satisfactions even those of unity . . . in order to always ask to suffer with him. He is honey to the soul, and rest and fire!' (14 August '48)

He was consolation, companionship, fullness, serenity, love.

'And you . . . don't forget Jesus Forsaken. When everything in your life disappears, you will find him again, faithfully faithful: he, the betrayed, to console all who are betrayed; the failure, to console all who have failed; the emptiness, to fill every emptiness; the sorrowing one, to brighten every sorrow; the unloved, who replaces – in a divine way – every love which has been lost or has not been found. Love him in the inner cell of your heart that is, and will remain, completely and always only his.' (20 August '49)

He was a 'heavenly' love – this was the adjective we used: this is what God wanted for us.

'Our love, that love which must reign in our hearts, must be because Jesus wants it to be so, a heavenly love, a love that is always joyful! . . . Let's not offend . . . this Love with complaints or feelings of dejectedness but let's always be ready to overcome every suffering with joy and in joy, because this is God's will for us, and we have all the grace, it's enough that we know how to use it.' (8 December '44)

Living in this way we experience full joy. Here are some testimonies.

'Prefer among all moments (of the day) those that are painful (especially the abandonments we experience in the soul) because there it is Jesus crucified and forsaken who "marries" the soul.

'This preference which initially is always a matter of the will, soon becomes a matter of our affections and then one throws oneself into a sea of suffering and one finds oneself in a sea of love, of full joy. We have seen through our continual experience that every suffering of the soul (not of the body[10]) can be cancelled and the soul feel itself full of the Holy

---

[10] Experiences of the first stages of the spiritual life in the way of unity are presented here. They are valid also for the later stages, with the exception of certain particular moments and periods, as will be indicated below.

Spriti, who is joy, peace, serenity . . . I always have more and more light about this possibility of conquering the death of the soul (that is, privation of love, of light, of joy, of peace) with life which is *Christ crucified and forsaken*!' (23 April '45)

'[You have been] tested by pain and you know that the flower of true joy is born only from a ground of suffering. Today and only today I've learned that suffering is the condition for that unique joy which can be born in a heart that follows Christ.' (29 June '45)

In 1945 we already knew the way to love Jesus Forsaken.

'Our soul is either in joy or is in suffering. When the soul does not sing something is worrying it and that something should immediately be given to God. There can be sufferings on account of external things . . . there can be inner sufferings (scruples doubts, dejectedness, temptation, emptiness, nostalgia). All these sufferings are to be given to God. The swifter the gift, the sooner love descends into our hearts.

'If you feel something, whatever it is, which does not leave your soul in peace, you must give this something to him . . . If you keep something for yourself, even only the thought of the gift you have given, you take possession of a richness (a mean richness) which is no longer yours.' (15 April '45)

And we explained how by doing this, we annulled

suffering. It was necessary, however, to turn ourselves at once to living well and fully, the will of God in the following moment.

In another letter, indeed, we read:

'However, I want you to know, Father, that it is absolutely not part of our vocation to suffer pains of the soul. They will come. But we must overcome them and we can always do this. All that's needed is that it is enough that Jesus Forsaken is everything for us . . .

Rejoice to suffer with him and *continue to love him by doing his will*. Sufferings pass. Our vocation is unity, the fullness of joy.' (10 May '48)

In 1945 it became more clear that the joy which fills the soul is like a triumphal entry of God, like a true Easter. We will see later how appropriate this definition is.

'. . . only in the extreme poverty of the soul, which loses itself for love, does God make his triumphal entry with the fullness of joy. This is why Easter was for us a "passage" to a life that is joy which will never end, for as long as we live according to our chosen ideal.

'Do you now want our Eternal Model? Jesus crucified and forsaken. His soul, the soul of the God-Man, filled with the greatest pain ever known by heaven and earth, the suffering of a God forsaken by God, his soul does not hesitate for a moment to offer this suffering to his Father: 'Father, into your hands I commend my spirit!' (Luke 23:46) This is what we too must always do. And do you know how Jesus will respond to your offering? He will give you everything, all the fullness of his joy.' (15 April '45)

And it is possible to see how the fruit of this love for Jesus Forsaken is to be Jesus, to live Jesus.

'I want to give you the latest development of our thoughts, so that the light of love may shine in you more brightly . . . Take . . . every moment all that is yours and give it to him. Give it to him always more quickly. The quicker you give it to him, the sooner you'll be him. What greater thing can I say to you? And what is life in love, if not to be a copy of him? If not to live him? Here is our sanctity: to arrive at being him. To be able to say with St Paul, "It is no longer I who live, but it is Christ who lives in me."' (Gal. 2:20) (22 April '45)

Jesus Forsaken drew us like a magnet, so that from the very first months (that is, still in 1944) we were attracted to put ourselves in the very depths of his forsaken heart, where we identified our place as being in his wound, which we called 'new' because we thought it was little known, and had not yet been examined profoundly enough. And, having entered, as we used to say 'beyond the wound' (that is: having completely embraced Jesus Forsaken in such a way as to find oneself beyond suffering, in love) it seemed to us that we were contemplating the immense love of God poured out on the world.

In fact, it is from the suffering of the Crucified one, which reaches its climax in that cry, that redemption, sanctification, and deification, come.

'Beyond the wound' we understood truly what Love is, we were merged with love and we shared in its light: the light of Love.

This was a way of expressing the vocation we felt to pass through the abandonment, to find God, to find Love.

'We who follow this ideal the most beautiful, the most attractive ideal, have thrown ourselves with all our soul into the new wound of the abandonment! And in there we are secure, because we live in the heart of our Love. Not only this, but in there we see all the immensity of the Love of God which is poured out on the world. Put yourself too (in the wound) . . . ! You will find the light of love (and, that is) it will be explained to you what Love is, because Jesus is the light of the world.' (8 December '44)

To sum up: supernatural life, virtue, sweetness, fire, rest, consolation, fullness, companionship, peace, serenity, love, heavenly love, the light of Love, Love, Jesus, God – these are the extraordinary fruits of this life, of love for Jesus Forsaken when, in this embrace – as we said above – he 'marries the soul'.

A well-known passage says:

'Jesus Forsaken embraced, held tightly to oneself, desired as our one exclusive all, he consumed in *one* with us, we consumed in *one* with him, made suffering with him suffering: here is everything. This is how you become (by participation) God, Love.' (1949)

And today, after forty years of the life of our Movement, these effects persist, indeed they are an everyday matter.

We experience in our hearts, with the deepest gratitude to God, this continual flowering of Life which is always new; we witness in our own souls continuous dawnings of light, which clear everything away: doubts, torments, worries, putting the shadows to flight. We can be filled with such heavenly joys that we are moved in our very depths, so that nothing remains but to offer to God throughout the day holocausts of rejoicing: we are aware that the Holy Spirit is not distant but extremely close, and he enlightens and guides us.

And even persons who are not part of the Work of Mary often notice these realities in the members of the Movement.

Important figures in all the Christian Churches, who have to travel throughout the world, sometimes say that they can distinguish the members of the Movement by the fruits of the Spirit which they believe they can see on their faces; and say they have been struck, for example, not only by the witness of reciprocal love which they give but particularly by their joy.

III

We have, therefore, examined what we discovered in Jesus Forsaken in the early times of our Movement; we have seen where we found him, what our attitude towards him had to be and we have underlined, in the end, the various effects produced by love for him.

Today we ask ourselves: what are these effects? How can these fruits be classified?

When we spoke of unity, of our life of communion with our brothers and sisters, we understood that unity is Jesus, is the Risen One. In unity 'you feel, you see, you enjoy the presence of Jesus. Everyone rejoices in his presence, everyone suffers from his absence. It is peace, joy, love, ardour, the atmosphere of heroism, of the highest generosity . . .' And these effects, this atmosphere, are the fruit of the Spirit of Jesus, that is, the Holy Spirit himself. And the Spirit of the Risen Jesus in our midst enables us to be Jesus, and we appear to others too as a continuation of him, the Body of Christ, Church.

In fact, whoever builds unity with mutual love, lives Christ's death and his resurrection: that person 'experiences' the life of the Risen One, which he has within himself through grace. He lives, therefore, the life that does not die. Jesus says: '. . . everyone who lives and believes in me will never die.' (John 11:26)

But we have noticed that also in the embracing of Jesus Forsaken, which each Christian can do, one experiences effects which are equal to those experienced in unity. Indeed, one experiences identical effects.

What must we conclude? While accepting that each Christian is not and can never be an isolated person, can we deduce that also in each one of us singly, if we have embraced Jesus Forsaken, the Risen One makes himself present, with the same intensity, strength, power, totality with which he is among us in full unity?

Let us see what the Church thinks about it.

First of all let us try to understand if there is a relationship between Jesus crucified and forsaken and the gift of the Holy Spirit.

The Gospel of St John says, 'When Jesus had received the wine, he said, "It is finished". Then he bowed his head and gave up his spirit.' (John 19:30)

The theologian Lyonnet commented on this passage thus: 'John's expression in speaking of the death of Jesus "Then he bowed his head and gave up his spirit" (John 19:30) is unusual. The verb "gave up" (delivered) (the spirit) seems chosen to indicate the voluntary offering of his life on the part of Christ . . . Using a completely unusual expression to indicate the death of Jesus, John wished to tell us that the death had as its effect the giving of the Spirit to the community.'[11]

In an Italian Ecumenical translation of the Bible we read: 'John wished to suggest that by means of his death Jesus can transmit the Spirit to the world.'

And Yves Congar writes, '. . . Jesus breathes on Mary and John who are like the Church at the foot of his cross. Jesus transmits the Spirit . . . Many Fathers have understood it thus.'[12]

St Jerome, commenting on John 7:39 states: 'The Spirit had not yet been given, because Jesus had not yet been glorified, that is, had not yet been crucified.'[13]

St Ambrose noted that, 'Jesus crucified, thirsting, pierced through, open rock from which water flows, fulfils what he promised in John 7:38. "In that moment therefore he was thirsty, when from his side poured out rivers of living water which would quench the thirst of all".'[14] (Water symbolizes the spirit.)

St Paul says that Jesus became cursed in the (death on the) cross so that we could receive the promise of the Spirit (cf. Gal 3:13ff).

---

[11] S. Lyonnet, *Il Nuovo Testamento alla luce dell'Antico*, Brescia 1970, p. 92, cit. in *Il Vangelo di Giovanni*, a commentary by B. Maggioni, in *Il Vangelo*, Assisi 1975, pp. 1671–72.
[12] Yves Congar, *Je crois en l'Esprit Saint*, I, Paris 1979, p. 79.
[13] Quoted by H. Rahner, *L'ecclesiologia dei Padri*, Rome, 1971, p. 380.
[14] Ibid. p. 338.

In the encyclical *Mystici Corporis* we read, 'through his blood . . . the Church became enriched with that most abundant communication of the Spirit . . .'

'He is the Spirit who Christ merited for us on the cross with the shedding of his blood.'[15] 'And since Christ has been glorified on the Cross his Spirit is communicated to the Church in abundant outpouring.'[16] The relationship between Jesus crucified and the Spirit is clear: Jesus gained it for us on the cross. But, obviously, the cross of Jesus coincides with his forsakenness: if being forsaken was one of the sufferings of Jesus on the cross – indeed, it is the peak of Jesus' sufferings – it is impossible to speak of his sufferings, of the cross, without thinking of the forsakenness. To say, then, that there is a relationship between the cross of Jesus and the Holy Spirit is also to say that there is a relationship between Jesus crucified and forsaken and the Holy Spirit.

Nonetheless (even though it is not yet stated by others), we can perhaps think that that particular suffering of Jesus, which is his forsakenness, has a special relationship with the Holy Spirit.

And we can think this simply because when you give something you necessarily feel the lack of it.

---

[15] Pius XII, *Mystici Corporis*, 30 and 54 (Trans. Canon George D. Smith).
[16] Ibid.

Jesus on the cross in that tremendous moment experienced detachment from the Father. But is it not precisely the Holy Spirit who bound him and who binds him to the Father in personal communion?

A theologian writes:

'In the sacred texts the coming of the Holy Spirit is placed in intimate relationship with the mystery of the passage of Christ to the Father. Within this mystery, in fact, comes about the most perfect realization of the human love of the incarnate Word, the sign of the spirant love from which the Divine Spirit proceeds.'[17]

But if the climax of the love of Jesus crucified, is the abandonment, in this cry there is 'the most perfect realization of the human love of the incarnate Word'. Thus we can think that in the abandonment there is 'the sign of the spirant love from which the Divine Spirit proceeds'.

In any case, that there is a relationship between Jesus crucified and forsaken and the gift of the Holy Spirit is a matter beyond doubt.

And now let us go a step further. Is the Holy Spirit which is given by Jesus through the cross, given only to the community or also to persons singly?

Jesus said: '"Let anyone who is thirsty come to me, and let the one who believes in me drink. As the

[17] M. Bordoni, *Il tempo: valore filosofico e mistero teologico*, Rome 1965, pp.141–42.

scripture has said, 'Out of the believer's heart shall flow rivers of living water.'" Now this he said about the Spirit, which believers in him were to receive.' (John 7:37–39)

Out of 'his heart': thus, the heart of the single person.

We read in St Basil: 'The Holy Spirit is present in each of those who receive him, as if he were conferred upon him alone.'[18]

Congar says: 'The Holy Spirit is given to the community and to individuals.'[19]

These testimonies are enough to assure us that the Crucified Lord gives the Holy Spirit also to Christians singly.

We know what the Holy Spirit does in each one of us.

St Paul says: '[God] even when we are dead through our trespasses, made us alive together with Christ – by grace you have been saved – and raised us up with him, and seated us with him in the heavenly places in Christ Jesus.' (Eph. 2:5–6)

Congar says: 'During Jesus' human life the Holy Spirit had in him his temple that contained all humankind in the expectancy and in the potential state of their assumption as children of God. After the Lord's glorification, the Holy Spirit has this

---

[18] St. Basil, *Liber de Spirito Sancto,* IX, 22.
[19] Yves Congar, *Credo nello Spirito Santo*, II, Brescia 1982, pp. 22 & 25.

temple in us and in the Church. He fulfils in us the same work of birth (*anothen*: from above, anew, John 3:3), of life as members of the body of Christ, of the consummation of this quality in our very own body, in the glory and the freedom of the children of God (Rom. 8: 21–23).'[20]

A theologian states: 'In baptism the faithful are united to Christ dead and risen. In their intimate and real union, while living in this world, they share in the heavenly triumph on the mystical plane of grace and they await the manifestations of glory. Christians re-awakened to a new life and ideally in heaven, have changed their former being into a new one, that is, into the being of Christ. This radical change has come about by the clothing themselves in Christ and sharing in his destiny.'[21]

Hence it is true that, through Jesus crucified and forsaken who is embraced, the Holy Spirit is able to pour out his gifts fully also in each one of us: it is true that the Risen One can manifest himself in each one of us.

We had already understood that, through the life of grace and our mutual love, we were living unity fully, which is nothing other than the Risen One in our midst. Now we can affirm that, through the life

[20] Yves Congar, *op.cit.* pp.77–8.
[21] Elio Peretto, *Commento alla lettera agli 'Efesini' in Il Nuovo Testamento,* II Ed. Paoline, 1977, p. 654.

of grace, which is in each of us, and through embracing, Jesus crucified and forsaken, in each of us singly the Risen One can live with his Spirit, in such a way that we may experience the fruits.

Thus we can say with the theologian, Cardinal Ratzinger: 'The fount of the Spirit is Christ, the crucified. But, thanks to him, every Christian is a fount of the Spirit.'[22]

We can have a further proof of presence of the Holy Spirit in Christians, singly, and therefore of his fruits from the saints.

In fact, looking more closely at 'the will of God', we were able to note how these giants of religion, who accomplished the will of God by killing their own will (by embracing therefore the cross of renunciation and suffering) experienced, they say, 'an ineffable beatitude . . . peace, tranquillity and a really heavenly bliss', (St Frances Cabrini), 'peace and calm' (St Catherine of Siena), 'a continual celebration' (St Vincent de Paul). They experienced the fruits of the Spirit, among which is joy.

Joy! We mentioned joy in the first chapter, when speaking about unity. Now we have seen how joy is an effect of love for Jesus Forsaken, always because it is a fruit of the Spirit – joy which often manifests

[22] J. Ratzinger, *Lo Spirito Santo come «communio»*, in *La riscoperta dello Spirito Sancto*, Milan 1977, p.258.

the other fruits, which sums them up, and crowns them; joy which is the flower of love, expression of life, of fullness, of consolation, of happiness, of beatitude; that joy which witnesses the light in the soul . . .

It has been said that joy is the uniform of the focolarino. And this is so. It must be so. It cannot but be so, because the spirituality of the focolarino is unity and Jesus in his prayer for unity says: 'that they may have my joy made complete in themselves.' (John 17:13) Our joy, the joy of a Christian, in fact, is the joy of Jesus: not only the serene joy of children, certainly not the exuberance of the young which is simply human; nor is it good humour; it is not earthly happiness . . . Jesus has 'his' joy, just as he has 'his' peace.

God wants 'his' joy in the Christian, in the folcolarino.

While we must be thoughtful and serious and sorrowful with those who are so, normally we must be in joy, which is the open flower of love, the smile of love upon the world.

Every time that joy does not invade our hearts, we must ask ourselves: are we on the right road? Are we in the will of God?

But is joy always possible?

The testimonies that we have quoted are from early times of the Movement, hence they are the first experiences.

Now many years have passed and certainly we are more mature. What do we think today?

First of all it seems to us that we must affirm that this fullness of joy, through embracing Jesus Forsaken, is the norm of our life: just as we must experience in us the death of Christ, sharing in his passion, so we must experience in us his resurrection.

And the Spirit – we saw – has led us by the hand and suggested to us all that we needed to know so that this could become a reality in our life.

This experience of death and resurrection, then, is made possible for us in an easier way by our communitarian vocation by our travelling together towards God. We will never be able to evaluate the help our brothers and sisters give us, even without our knowing it. How much courage their faith infuses in us, how much warmth their love, how we are drawn ahead by their example! We will never know how to calculate the strength the presence of Christ in the community puts into us.

There can, however, be particular moments, periods in life that are special, in which it is all but impossible to make joy penetrate in our heart, despite all our good will and sincere embracing of Jesus Forsaken. They are dark moments, full of shadow, on account of the most varied spiritual pains, owing also to psycho-physical states, as we can often see to be the case. Or, more rarely, owing to true spiritual trials, genuine agonies, which the saints, for example, have experienced, and which are called 'nights of the senses' and 'nights of the spirit'. These are moments in which one is called to share the suffering of Jesus Forsaken in such a way as not to know how to say anything other than, '*Fiat*' – 'Thy will be done', with one's remaining strength. God permits them, as he permitted the abandonment his Son on the cross but in us it is for our purification and our sancitification and, at times, to associate us with the redemptive work of Jesus.

However, if these painful moments exist, generally they do not regard the normal life of the focolarini. The focolarini, whatever their spiritual age, are called to live in joy, to have so much joy that they communicate it to others. They are called to show to the world the Risen One in themselves, as well as among them.

With an example typical of the times in which we live, at a certain point in our history we said that Jesus Forsaken is like a machine: anyone who passes through him comes out another Jesus. And we exhorted one another not to remain in the machine, in suffering, but to allow the Risen One to shine out his life through us. Now, this is also true today: for the youngest who are just starting on the pathway, for the person who has known it for a while, for those who are or ought to be its teachers.

Sometimes it is possible to note, instead, that this joy does not exist, or that it is not full. And this is certainly not because Jesus Forsaken is visiting the soul with particular trials, but because we have perhaps ceased to make him the preferred and exclusive love of our life.

There is no resurrection without death. There is no joy of Jesus without love for Jesus Forsaken.

There is no joy of Jesus without loved suffering.

If we do not have the joy of the resurrection it means that Jesus Forsaken is no longer the ideal of our life, of our present moment. In his place there will be work, our self which wants to live when it must die, or study, activities, things, created beings.

In fact, the joy that God wishes to give us is special: it is the joy of the Risen Jesus, which blossoms on suffering, bursts out from renunciation, accompanies love.

And it is a contagious joy, which stands out, which is striking, which attracts, which converts. It is not an improvised joy, not a front you can put on to fool yourself or others.

To possess joy then, you must make and re-make the choice of him every day and love him all the day long: in the sufferings which come, in renunciations, in the mortifications demanded by our Christian life, and by our life as focolarini, and in the penances which we cannot overlook.

Love Jesus Forsaken so that Jesus may live in us. Jesus in the abandonment gave himself completely; in the spirituality which is centred on him, the Risen

Jesus must shine out fully and joy must witness to him.

In these chapters we have spoken of and quoted from several letters: they are the most numerous documents which have remained from the early times, which speak of Jesus Forsaken.
But, to whom were they written?

We wrote to our friends to draw them to the same ideal, to our parents and to other relatives, one by one: through them, also, we wanted to reach many others. We wrote to priests, to religious, to future religious. And as fire envelops all it meets, just as nothing and no-one is outside it but it grasps everything with its flames, so does the spiritual fire of these letters burn.

'Look at him there where he is crucified and think: if he had been your son? Hear him crying, "My God, my God, why have you forsaken me?"

'It is the cry that echoes every moment in my heart. Think of him dying almost in despair and nailed down like a lamb – poor Jesus! Go on . . . tell me that you too love him and you want to make him loved by others! Tell me that, if in life I should die first, you will make the flame of my heart yours. (25 December '44)

'In the name of him, crucified for Love for me and for you . . . accept my wish and make it yours: that love make you understand how much he loved you and does love you! And may love stir up in your heart my passion of Love.' (25 December '44)

'You too . . . hurry to love Jesus crucified and forsaken by everybody, even, by his Father . . . I want you to have my ideal which is him: Jesus Forsaken, and do everything that he may not be forsaken any longer, either by you or all those who pass your way in life.

'Look around you and see how many souls there are. Make the effort to make them love this Love, which must save the world. Become friends with your sister's friends and tell them to love this forsaken Love and everything else will be "added unto them". But "everything else" doesn't matter. What matters is only to love Love!' (undated)

God urged us, therefore, to open everyone's eyes. As everybody was a candidate for unity, everybody had to know the one who has paid for it, had to know who is the key to unity.

Nobody should remain indifferent, but all had to be aware of how much Jesus has loved us.

His cry was for *everyone*!

From the very beginning, in fact, our heart felt it had as it were a mission!

'. . . you know that my Love has called me to carry out a great mission.

'I must, I want to make him loved by all

the world, because for me he was crucified and forsaken!

'And you . . . have pity on this Jesus who continues to knock at your heart to have consolation from you!

'You must, you can embrace my ideal! Even if your way is a little different from mine.' (1 January '45).

We were moved, then, to speak about him to everybody.

We felt the vocation to create around him, as we said 'a paradise of stars'.

To a girl, to whom we gave the name Eli, we wrote as early as 1945:

'Cry out [which meant: live!] your name to the Eternal Father and to the heart of the Virgin! Cry it out for the whole of humanity, for every sinner of the world, for our girls . . . Cry it out from the depths of your heart. "But why, my God, have you forsaken me?"

'Cry it out as if you were Jesus, because the heavenly Father and the mother of Jesus and of us, cannot but come to our aid when they hear that cry! We have such great need of help from heaven to form on earth "a paradise of stars" for Jesus Forsaken!' (30 October '45)

Certainly, these moments to which the letters give witness were ones of a particular grace. But they are moments which perhaps in another way, we are called to relive today and we can do so fully if it is not we who live, but the Risen One lives in us. Through him we understood we too became founts of the Spirit. We too are other Jesuses. And if, this is true, his word: 'I came to bring fire to the earth' (Luke 12:49) becomes ours as well. We too can and must be fire for this world.

We must therefore announce Jesus Forsaken to all and we must extend the vineyard of Jesus Forsaken, which is our Movement, and make it flower in a better way: this is the concretization today of the 'paradise of stars' we mentioned before.

We must announce Jesus Forsaken, however, at the opportune moment. If, from the early times, the two faces of the medal of the Ideal have been Jesus Forsaken and unity, the Spirit urged us to proceed thus: to offer unity to others straightaway, while keeping Jesus Forsaken for ourselves.

'To everyone I show the page of unity. For myself and for those who are in the front line of unity, our one and only *all is Jesus forsaken* . . .

'To the others unity, for us the abandonment. Which abandonment?

'The one that Jesus . . . suffered . . . "My God, my God, why have you forsaken me?"

Our highest duty is to seek him like the bride in the Songs of Songs, we who have been cast by infinite love into the front line.' (30 March '48)

The first witness to give to the world is that of unity. Whoever is touched by it will then know how to grasp its secret.

Indeed, for anyone who chooses unity the encounter with Jesus Forsaken happens of necessity:

'Ah, brother! If you plunge yourself into this way (of unity), you will soon experience the stigmata of the abandonment! Then the Lord will dig in your heart an infinite void . . . which you will fill immediately with Jesus Forsaken.' (30 March '48)

With these suggestions full of wisdom the Holy Spirit set us out on our mission, the mission that the Movement has in the Church and the world: to contribute to *Ut omnes unum sint* (may they all be one) through the dialogue of love with everybody, a dialogue which is possible and constructive if it is preceded by witness. Dialogue, therefore, about Someone who has already been experienced, at least a little: God, who manifests himself in unity, so that we learn to discover his love in the incarnation, in the cross, in the abandonment, so that all of us may clothe ourselves in this love, and become identified with it, so that, we may radiate the Risen Jesus, more and more in the world.

Jesus Forsaken
Key to Unity with our Neighbours

Jesus Forsaken is not only the path, the key to the unity of our soul with God. He is also the key to unity with our neighbours, the key to the way to love them, the key to the manner for us to love one another.

And this is an essential topic for our Movement.

As we know, the choice of God-Love, from the moment this new life came to be, meant the choice of the way of love. In a truly divine synthesis, the Spirit made us recognize immediately all that Jesus desired from us in this characteristic commandment of his: 'I give you a new commandment, that you love one another.' (John 13:34)

Unity with other people, unity between people, is therefore a subject of extreme importance for us. It is not by chance that when we are asked who we are, we are often at a loss to find any better way of replying than telling the little story of our beginnings: the collapse of everything in wartime, the choice of God and, to live up to that choice, the practice of this commandment.

We always return to this command of Jesus as to the first and fundamental inspiration; it fascinates us, it attracts us, we rediscover it as new everytime we consider it in depth; living it we feel that we are in our element.

Enthusiasm grasps us, then, when we realize that if it is a subject of such great importance for us, little children of the church, it was also so for the Church when it began ('For this is the message *you have heard from the beginning*, that we should love one another,' 1 John 3:11), just as it is of great importance also for the Church today.

Vatican II specifies that the law of the new people of God is the commandment of love. In love, indeed, there is not just one law of Christ, but the whole of *his* law. Scripture has always affirmed that: 'the one who loves another has fulfilled the law.' (Rom. 13:8) For the whole law is summed up in a single commandment, 'You shall love your neighbour as yourself.' (Gal. 5:14).

Love, charity, participation in that *agape* which is God's own life ('God is *agape*', 1 John 4:8), is the highest mark of Christianity; in fact, it is the whole of our religion.

The Christian freed from all slavery by the Spirit who lives in him or her, through this Spirit, whose fruits are 'love, joy, peace, patience, kindness, generosity, faithfulness, gentleness' (Gal. 5:22–23), becomes the slave of someone: of his or her neighbours. The Christian lives life paying a perennial debt: that of serving other people (cf. Rom. 13:8).

And this love that Christ commands for neighbours, the service he commands, is not made up only of acts, one after another, but it is like a state which Christians must attain, a state which they must reach in the best way possible: their perfection. Service of one's neighbour, in fact, is the way *par excellence*, of Christian perfection. 'Love binds everything together in perfect harmony.' (Col. 3:14)

Although Vatican II gives the example of the vows of religious as an effective way of reaching sanctity it does not hesitate to place service of one's neighbour above them,[23] because love for one's neighbour is in truth the specific characteristic of the Christian: St Paul, moreover, puts charity above all the charisms. (Cf. 1 Cor. 13)

And so, if the Church thinks like this, if this is precisely how the Holy Spirit always taught us directly in our heart, we can understand how important it is to know the best way of loving our brothers and sisters, the most apt manner of accomplishing unity with them.

Jesus said: 'This is my commandment, that you love one another' but he did not leave this love without a model, for he added, 'as I have loved you.' (John 15:12) And he did not leave this love without any

[23] Cf. *Lumen Gentium*, 42.

explanation when he added further: 'No one has greater love than this, to lay down one's life for one's friends.' (John 15:13)

Yes, Jesus crucified and forsaken is the way of loving our neighbours. His death on the cross, forsaken, is the highest, divine, heroic lesson from Jesus about what love is.

This vision of Jesus crucified and forsaken is what the Holy Spirit has engraved on the hearts of the members of our Movement so that they may know what love is. It is to Jesus crucified and forsaken that, as much as their weakness permits, they conform their lives.

We saw, previously, how to love means to serve and how there is no better way of serving than 'to make ourselves one' with our neighbours.

No-one has made himself one with his neighbours like Jesus Forsaken. For this reason, he is the model of the person who loves, he is the way and the key to unity with our neighbours.

'To make ourselves one.'

But what is meant and what is demanded by these few short words, which are so important as to be the way of loving?

We cannot enter the spirit of other persons to understand them, to sympathize with them, to share their suffering, if our spirit is rich with a worry, a judgment, a thought . . . with anything at all. 'Making ourselves one' demands spirits that are poor, people who are poor in spirit. Only with people like this is unity possible.

And who, then, do we look to in order to learn this great art of being poor in spirit, this art which (as the Gospel says) brings with it the kingdom of God, the kingdom of love, love in the soul? We look to Jesus Forsaken. No-one is poorer than he: he, having lost nearly all of his disciples, having given his mother away, gives also his life for us and experiences the terrible sensation that the Father himself is abandoning him.

Looking at Jesus Forsaken we understand how everything is to be given or put aside for love of our neighbours: the things of this earth must be given or put aside and also – should it be necessary – in a certain way, the things of heaven. In fact, looking at him who felt himself forsaken by God, when love for other people asks us (and this can also happen often) to leave even God for God, as we say – (God, for example, in prayer, to 'to make ourselves one' with someone in need; God in that which seems to us to be our inspiration, to be completely empty, and to welcome into ourselves another's suffering), looking at him, every renunciation is possible.

And 'making ourselves one' involves this renunciation, even if we know what is to be gained by doing so. People who are loved in this way are often won over to Christ ('To the weak I became weak, that I might win the weak. I have become all things to all people, that I might by all means save some.' 1 Cor. 9:22) And, once they are won over, they too love and then, there is unity.

The Statute of the Movement says: 'The life of union among the faithful . . . will demand of its members a very special love for the cross and in particular for Jesus in the mystery of his passion: the divine model for all those who want to work together for the union of all with God and with one another, *the highest point of outer but above all of inner renunciation.*'[24] And it goes on to refer to the cry of Jesus: 'My God, my God, why have you forsaken me?'

It is Jesus Forsaken, therefore, who is the cause of unity.

Jesus Forsaken, however, is also the way to unity with our neighbours in another way.

Jesus said: 'I am in them and you in me, that they may become completely one.' (John 17:23)

---

[24] *General Statutes*, Rome 1962, part 1, chap. 1, art. 2–10. The revised Statutes, Rome 1990, say: 'In their commitment to live unity they look for and choose first and foremost Jesus crucified who in the height of his passion cried out, 'My God, my God, why have you forsaken me?' They see him as the way to unity with God and one another. Love for Jesus crucified and forsaken – the divine model for those who wish to work for unity – helps those who are part of the Focolare to have the outer and, even more importantly, the inner detachment necessary for there to be supernatural unity.

Thus, it is Jesus present in each Christian, who makes them perfect in unity.

We have looked in depth at this when we spoke about Jesus Forsaken, key to the unity of the soul with God. We should always embrace generously and without hesitation, Jesus Forsaken. who presents himself in the sufferings of each day, in the renunciations which the Christian life and all the virtues involve.

Then the Risen One, who we hope is already in us by grace, shines out in all his splendour; the gifts of the Spirit flow into our souls: it is an renewed Easter each time; Jesus lives in each one of us fully.

But if Jesus lives in me, and lives also in my neighbour, it is obvious that, when we meet, we are already one, we are perfect in unity.

And what has made all this possible? Love for Jesus Forsaken.

Jesus Forsaken is also the way of unity with our neighbours because he helps to rebuild unity each time it is shattered. In fact it can happen that we have already experienced that full joy, that peace, that light, that ardour, that inclination to love, all those fruits of the Spirit which are produced by the New Commandment when it is put into practice. It may be, that is, that we already know what is meant by the presence of Jesus among two or more Christians who are united in his name. And we may have experienced what tremendous meaning it has given to our existence, even in its details: how it has shed light on circumstances, things and people. But all of a sudden, an act of pride, arrogance or a speck of selfishness on the part of one person or the other, makes us plunge back into an existence similar to that which we had before knowing Jesus more fully, an existence without warmth and colour, and even worse than that. An uneasiness invades the soul; everything loses meaning: we do not understand why we set out on this way. The most important element is missing: He who made our life full, who had made us brim-over with joy, is missing. It is as if a supernatural sun had set.

What are we to do?

In that moment only the memory of the black forsakenness into which his divine soul had been plunged, can be light for us. Would not the fact that Jesus had lived all his life for the Father, have lost its value for him if, at the climax of his offering, the Father abandoned him? What sense was there in dying now? But he did not doubt: 'Father, into your hands I commend my spirit!' (Luke 23:46)

At such a moment, troubled in our souls by the small or large disunity, and aware of sharing a little of that agony of his, we go to the full depth of our heart and we embrace our suffering and then: we run to our brother or sister to rebuild full harmony – whether we or they were responsible for what happened. (The Gospel, when it asks us not to bring our gift to the altar before being reconciled with our brother or sister, does not distinguish between guilty and not guilty.) And Jesus returns among us, bringing with him strength and happiness again.

Jesus Forsaken is always the key to every unity that is re-established.

Jesus in his abandonment is the way to unity with our neighbours also in another way which is mysterious, but real.

He said: 'I, when I am lifted up from the earth, will draw all people to myself', (John 12:32); that is, I will make all one.

If it is true that Christ lives in the Christian, the Christian can, in a certain way, repeat this word about himself. We do not know how much has been contributed to unity in our Movement by all those living crucifixes who, day by day, are raised by God's will upon the cross of short or long illnesses or even deaths offered for our Movement. God knows. Certainly their gift is always of tremendous worth if, in the divine economy, suffering is the most fruitful element.

But who do all these people look to, who offer for the aims of the Movement their Mass as a continuation of his? They look at him, to whose Passion they unite their own, so that all 'may be one'.

Jesus Forsaken, lastly, is the cause of our unity with our neighbours also because we see him, some semblance of him, in all those who suffer. We see him in those who are troubled, in those rejected by society, in the persecuted, in the needy, in those who suffer hunger and thirst, in the naked, the sick, the dying, in the homeless. We see him in prisoners: who is more a prisoner and pinned down than he, in a bodily sense but also in his soul, because of the terrifying sensation that he has been abandoned by the Father with whom he is perfectly one?

We see him in those in doubt. What greater doubt than his when, for us, he seems to believe the most absurd of absurdities: that God forsakes God?

We see him in the afflicted, in the unconsoled, in the forsaken, in failures, in the betrayed, in outcasts, in the victims of failures or of impossible situations, in the disorientated, in the defenceless or the desperate or those drowned in fear . . .

We see him also in the sinner, because for us he made himself sin, a curse (cf. Gal. 3:13).

In all of these persons, in all those who suffer in the soul and in the body, it is not difficult to recognize his face. And because we see his face, we love him.

Thus, his figure, that these suffering created beings recall, is the cause of our love. Jesus Forsaken is the way to unity with them. And they, then, once loved, more often than not, love in their turn. And behold, we have unity again.

Hence it is very understandable that the members of the Movement, because they love Jesus Forsaken, are open to love the whole of humanity and to direct it where they meet it towards *'ut omnes'*, 'may they all be one'.

Indeed, they feel the need of this love for him so strongly that it has become a practice for all of them, for decades now, to 'consecrate themselves' to Jesus Forsaken. Those who have greater responsibility do so, like the focolarini, the priests, the religious, the married people, the volunteers. The young people do as well. Even the children do so.

They all understand that here is the key of their Ideal.

They vow themselves, therefore, to Jesus Forsaken as the way of making explicit their vowing themselves to love, because he is Love.

But the Movement loves Jesus Forsaken in humanity not only in its members singly, but also as a whole and in its different parts. The various mass movements, for example, love Jesus Forsaken in the respective problems they deal with, which always manifest one of his faces.

Thus, for him, the New Families Movement finds itself successfully coping with the problems of orphans: who is more the figure of an orphan than Jesus in that moment on the cross? Or coping with widows: who, more than he, is alone, without protection or company? And likewise also for the problems of separation, of divorce, of the elderly, of the lack of communication between the generations etc.

For him, the New Humanity Movement strives to solve the thousands and thousands of humanity's problems in its various worlds: in the world of work – the problems of unemployment, of tension between social classes etc; in the world of politics – the problem of human rights, of the relationships between parties and so on.

For him, it works to give a reply to the problems of the world of health and of the school: who is more like those in need of instruction, than Jesus, the Word of God, who for us made himself ignorance with his 'why'?

For him, the Priests' Movement offers a solution to the problems of priests, of those who are too lonely or are old, to the problem of the insufficient communion which sometimes is found among them; the problem of their duty to be united with the bishops; to the problems of vocations, of seminaries . . . The Parish Movement seeks to respond to all of the problems presented by the Church in a parish, with its liturgical events, with its multiplicity of activities and its associations, but especially with the need it bears within itself to be a living community.

For him, the Movements of the Religious (Men and Women) know how to offer an answer to the many problems of religious families: the renewal of their spirit; the return to the observance of the Rule;

unity between the religious and with their superiors; vocations; unity between the various religious families.

For him, the young people's Movements (the Gen, the New Youth Movement . . .) give a hand to solve the grave problems of young people and children today.

The Focolare Movement, however – and this needs to be underlined – does not have as its direct aim the renewal of the family, youth, or the various worlds of society. Nor does it have as its direct goal that of solving the problems of religious families, of priests, of seminarians, of parishes . . . even though, in practice, it contributes towards solving and renewing all of these.

The aim of the Focolare Movement is to contribute towards the realization of the last will and testament of Jesus, in the world. To accomplish this end it has mass movements (which aim at youth, families, parishes, society, priests, religious): to create, to form a single tissue of the various components of the Christian world and to show to the world how the Church is when Christ, the Risen One, is in the midst of his children.

It is in this way, above all, through this witness of unity, with Christ present and his Spirit which renews everything (a witness which comes before any other apostolic activity) that the Movement feels it has the possibility of sharing with the Church its current concerns and its sufferings.

For us the various areas of the countries of the Third World to which the Church gives so much care and attention (where there are many necessities or possibilities, and few workers) are an echo of the cry of Jesus Forsaken to which we attempt in some way to respond.

Likewise, for our heart the Church of Silence is like one great Jesus crying out his forsakenness. We never forget what a bishop from one of those countries said, when he heard us speaking of this aspect of Jesus' passion: 'Jesus Forsaken is how the Church lives its passion today.'

And so we come to the three, possibly the three most important, objectives of the Church today, for which, after the Second Vatican Council, it has opened three great dialogues.

In the course of its forty years history, the Movement has also seen in these objectives its principal aims: the unification of Christians; dialogue with other religions; the dialogue linked with the very wide-spread problem of atheism in the world.

The Movement's spirituality (and this is a discovery we have been making through experience) contains in itself extremely useful elements for dialogue with the various Churches. And these have enabled us to open and to develop a constructive conversation with Christians of various denominations, so that a truly ecumenical reality has been born. These elements are: *love* as the central element of Christianity and *life* ('Yours is a way of life,' said Pope John Paul II) which have touched our Orthodox brothers and sisters; *the word of God* which we stress in a very special way, and which has opened for us a dialogue and a communion, which is also deep, with the Lutherans; *unity*, which has particularly interested our Anglican brothers and sisters, starting from those in authority in their Church; Jesus' words, '*Where two or more are met together in my name, there am I in their midst,*' which has been the key-word in our dialogue with members of the Reformed Churches, and so on.

Because of these various elements, which we have in common with Christians of other Churches or ecclesial communities, our Movement has been able to gather abundant fruit, such as, the collapse of centuries old prejudice on either side, the acceptance of truths of the Catholic Church on the part of other Christians, and in us more objective evaluation of many situations and in everyone a desire for unity which is often overwhelming.

But it has been above all through Jesus Forsaken that we have been able to construct something in this field.

We have always seen his disfigured figure (Jesus Forsaken in terrible anguish because of the uncertainty, so to speak, of his unity with the Father, appears really to be like the anti-figure of he who was always so certain of that unity), his disfigured figure in the Christian world which is called to the most perfect unity and at present is divided up into hundreds of Churches.

It is for him, for his cry which is raised up by so many traumas, divisions, separations, that the Movement feels itself mobilized to work to recompose unity in the Church.

The Movement, by spreading all over the world, has come into contact often with the faithful of other religions: with Jews, with Muslims, with Buddhists, with Taoists, with Sikhs, with Hindus etc. And with all of them we have found a motivation for a link.

If the priceless inheritance of the Old Testament, unites us to the Jews, and the Muslims find our living the faith not only singly but as a community something interesting on account of their idea of religious life, with the faithful of Eastern Religions we are bound in a special way by Jesus Forsaken. The others, too, are curious about Jesus Forsaken, we have often heard Jews affirm, after having come to know this culmination of Jesus' passion, 'Then, he was truly God.' (Cf. Mark 15:39)

But to the faithful of the Eastern Religions that typical suffering of Jesus, which, brought him to utter self-annihilation, brings to life a very particular fascination. Often, in fact, they seek that 'energy' (as they call it) which is beneath everything, or God, whom they love, sometimes as a person, by means of the mortification of their senses and every desire. And their asceticism is admirable. It carries them so high that when they meet genuine Christians, they are able to have a certain perception of Christian supernatural life. It is 'being', in fact, which has value for them. And when someone dies to self in order 'to make himself one' with them and consequently lets Christ live in himself, or when they came into contact with the Risen One in the midst of united Christians, which is also the fruit of love for the cross, they know how to distinguish that light and that peace, the effects of the Spirit, which shine from their face: they are attracted and they ask for an explanation. This leads to speaking of our religion: dialogue which becomes evangelization.

And there is the third dialogue, one which is also very special, to which the Movement feels itself called. It is the dialogue with non-believers, with those who are furthest away, with atheists, with materialists.

We believe, in fact, that it would have been meaningless for our Movement to have been called to make Jesus' greatest suffering its own, if it were not to have dedicated itself, in the midst of humanity, to the most wretched of all people.

And the most wretched, the most destitute are not even those who are dying of hunger; rather they are those who, after this life, will not know the other life, because they have rejected God or because they have put material things in God's place.

To dedicate ourselves to them, whom we find not only in countries which are well-known for being atheist, but who can be met in the West as in the East, in big cities as in little villages, is, it seems to us, the supreme call of our Movement; a call which is so characteristically ours, so special, that it makes us think of other dialogues, like that with non-Catholic Christians, are made to serve this one.

And so, to love. To love all people so that all may know the nature of love and may love one another as Jesus desired – this is the burning desire of our Movement.

Hence in the times in which it has been born, times caressed by the powerful currents of the breath of the Holy Spirit, but also threatened by atomic warfare, the Movement has its secret: Jesus Forsaken, he who bound human beings to God again and to one another. With its spirituality centred around Jesus Forsaken, a true 'divine atomic energy', as our Gen call it (it seems in that cry indeed that unity itself, which is God, is shattered; it is God who cries out: 'My God, my God why have you forsaken me?'), with this spirituality the Movement feels it can live in unison with the Church today and can pursue with the Church its goal which is for today and forever: to fulfil Jesus' last will and testament: 'May they all be one.' (John 17:21)